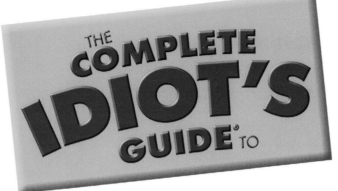

THE COMPLETE **IDIOT'S** GUIDE® TO

The Perfect Wedding *Illustrated*

Fifth Edition

by Teddy Lenderman

ALPHA

A member of Penguin Group (USA) Inc.

For Robert, the memories, adventures, and all the times to come,
I thank you.

ALPHA BOOKS

Published by the Penguin Group

Penguin Group (USA) Inc., 375 Hudson Street, New York, New York 10014, U.S.A.

Penguin Group (Canada), 10 Alcorn Avenue, Toronto, Ontario, Canada M4V 3B2 (a division of Pearson Penguin Canada Inc.)

Penguin Books Ltd, 80 Strand, London WC2R 0RL, England

Penguin Ireland, 25 St Stephen's Green, Dublin 2, Ireland (a division of Penguin Books Ltd)

Penguin Group (Australia), 250 Camberwell Road, Camberwell, Victoria 3124, Australia (a division of Pearson Australia Group Pty Ltd)

Penguin Books India Pvt Ltd, 11 Community Centre, Panchsheel Park, New Delhi—110 017, India

Penguin Group (NZ), cnr Airborne and Rosedale Roads, Albany, Auckland 1310, New Zealand (a division of Pearson New Zealand Ltd)

Penguin Books (South Africa) (Pty) Ltd, 24 Sturdee Avenue, Rosebank, Johannesburg 2196, South Africa

Penguin Books Ltd, Registered Offices: 80 Strand, London WC2R 0RL, England

International Standard Book Number: 978-1-59257-566-4
Library of Congress Catalog Card Number: 2006930728

3 9547 00295 6048

08 07 06   8 7 6 5 4 3 2 1

Interpretation of the printing code: The rightmost number of the first series of numbers is the year of the book's printing; the rightmost number of the second series of numbers is the number of the book's printing. For example, a printing code of 06-1 shows that the first printing occurred in 2006.

Printed in the United States of America

Note: This publication contains the opinions and ideas of its author. It is intended to provide helpful and informative material on the subject matter covered. It is sold with the understanding that the author and publisher are not engaged in rendering professional services in the book. If the reader requires personal assistance or advice, a competent professional should be consulted.

The author and publisher specifically disclaim any responsibility for any liability, loss, or risk, personal or otherwise, which is incurred as a consequence, directly or indirectly, of the use and application of any of the contents of this book.

Most Alpha books are available at special quantity discounts for bulk purchases for sales promotions, premiums, fund-raising, or educational use. Special books, or book excerpts, can also be created to fit specific needs.

For details, write: Special Markets, Alpha Books, 375 Hudson Street, New York, NY 10014.

Publisher: *Marie Butler-Knight*

Editorial Director: *Mike Sanders*

Executive Editor: *Randy Ladenheim-Gil*

Managing Editor: *Billy Fields*

Senior Development Editor: *Christy Wagner*

Production Editor: *Megan Douglass*

Copy Editor: *Jan Zoya*

Design and Layout: *Becky Harmon*

Proofreader: *Mary Hunt*

Contents at a Glance

Part 1: Don't Spend a Dime Yet!   2

1   Taking Your First Steps Toward the Altar   4
    Finding a system and keeping yourself organized.

2   Simple or Extravagant? Setting Your Budget   12
    Looking at the bottom line and determining what kind of wedding you can afford.

Part 2: First Things First   22

3   Get Me a Church on Time!   24
    Setting your date and finding a site for your ceremony.

4   Seeking Your Soirée   40
    Locating a facility and making the arrangements for your reception.

5   The Wedding Party: A Circle of Friends   52
    Asking your friends to share in your big day.

6   Cast Party: Arranging the Rehearsal Dinner   64
    Pulling together a relaxing and successful rehearsal dinner.

Part 3: Putting It All Together   72

7   Eat, Drink, and Be Married   74
    The nitty-gritty of planning the food and drink at your reception.

8   All Dressed Up and Somewhere to Go   90
    Tips to help the entire wedding party dress for success.

9   Snapdragons and Song   106
    Choosing the right florist and musicians.

10 Pretty as a Picture: Photographers and Videographers   122
    Putting all your wedding memories in the right hands.

11 Extra! Extra! Read All About It!   136
    Setting the right tone with your invitations, plus all the little things that can make your wedding special, such as programs and newsletters.

12 Do Yourself a Favor   150
    Great ideas and guidelines for favors, welcome baskets, and attendant gifts.

13 Let the Party Begin!   160
    Determining your reception agenda—what to include and when to include it.

14 Making the Most of Your Dollars   172
    Some ways to cut costs from your wedding budget without anyone ever knowing.

Part 4: Circling the Wagons: Preparing for the
         Main Event   182

15 And in This Corner ...   184
    *Emotional issues surrounding a wedding can cause tension between mothers
    and daughters.*

16 I Think I'm Losing My Mind!   194
    Reasons why you might sometimes feel like you're riding an emotional roller coaster.

17 Much Ado About Everything: Prenuptial Preparation   202
    Preparing for the big day.

Part 5: Extra Special Weddings   212

18 What's in a Theme?   214
    *Some different wedding ideas to help you let your imagination run wild, as
    well as ideas for having a weekend wedding.*

19 Mickey and Minnie, Here We Come: Destination Weddings   228
    Taking your wedding show on the road.

Appendixes
    A Wedding Worksheets   238
    B Countdown to Your Wedding Day   257

Foreword

Fifth editions of books in *The Complete Idiot's Guide* series are rare. That makes this edition of *The Complete Idiot's Guide to the Perfect Wedding Illustrated* very special—and for good reason.

Teddy Lenderman is the role model for bridal consultants, a true professional, and a superb storyteller. In this updated edition, she has done what many would consider impossible—taken the best and made it better! The format has changed. It's brighter, bolder, and has many more photos. Nevertheless, the core information still is here, and that core information is priceless.

When the Association of Bridal Consultants was founded in 1981, the wedding business was a sleepy cottage industry worth about $16 billion a year. There was no coordination: florists didn't know what the photographers were doing; the caterers didn't know the color scheme, etc. And bridal consultants? Except for the rich and famous, no one knew they existed.

Teddy joined the Association in 1986, one of approximately 120 members. Membership now is approximately 4,000 in almost 30 countries on 6 continents. Estimates place the industry's 2005 value at more than $125 billion. And everything is coordinated, presenting a wedding that meshes all aspects into a seamless, glorious event—at all budget levels. All these details fall into place in Teddy's coordinated, seamless, glorious book. She takes all the complexities of today's weddings, from the challenges of extended families (just where does the bride's stepfather's stepmother sit in the church?) and the mobile society (what are you going to do with all these people who have traveled long distances and are here for the entire weekend?), and presents the solutions in a clear, easy-to-read, lively manner.

Weddings are a rite of passage, just like birth and death ... but they are the only major one you can control. That's why couples spend so much money on them and why they are so significant.

Add to all this the fact that the traditional wedding planners—the bride herself, mothers, sisters, and aunts—probably are working and can't spend the 80 or more hours it takes to pull all this together. You need help. That's where Teddy, other wedding professionals, and this book come in. If you choose to do it all yourself, this will be an invaluable guide. If you do hire a wedding consultant (wise move!), read on, for you will find in these pages the wit and wisdom you will need to ask intelligent questions, things to help you and your coordinator do just that—coordinate.

I first met Teddy at an informal Association dinner in Indianapolis in July 1986. Her personality filled the room the same way it fills these pages. She has developed her business, Bearable Weddings and Special Events, into a recognized industry leader. She served for many years as the Association of Bridal Consultants' Indiana state coordinator, providing local information, networking, and mentoring, helping many get started in the business. She has presented seminars at the Association's Business of Brides annual conference and at The Special Event. An early leader in wedding education, she is a Master Bridal Consultant™—the highest educational designation the Association offers—one of only 35 in the world. And she was the first recipient of the "Miss Dorothy Heart Award," the only award the Association presents, for her passion for weddings. If these aren't good enough reasons to read this book, there is one more: it's fun!

Gerard J. Monaghan
Co-founder and former president
Association of Bridal Consultants
New Milford, Connecticut

Introduction

Today's weddings continue to be as different as the couples being married. Using the couple's uniqueness and developing a theme from that is a big trend. No two weddings are alike anymore. The average age of the bride and groom today is 26 and 28, respectively. Today's wedding couples are more mature, have their careers well in place, and are eager to get the planning process started. Many times the couple pays for the wedding and reception themselves or split it with one or both sets of parents. There are all kinds of options out there for the engaged couple, from having a weekend wedding to flying off to an exotic destination-wedding site, to the traditional wedding at home. Many couples plan their weddings from long distance. Whatever your plans or ideas, it sometimes seems very overwhelming.

Thousands of complex wedding-related questions are just lurking out there, waiting to be answered. It's hard to know where to go or whom to turn to for help. You've never done this kind of event before. Even if you're a vice president of a huge corporation, you start thinking, I must be an idiot. I don't have the faintest idea where to begin!

Well, you're not an idiot—not even close. You are, however, about to become a wedding consumer. You will have lots of questions, and you will need many, many answers. You deserve honest answers to your questions and some guidance from someone who knows this industry inside and out. You also deserve to be treated with respect by vendors. This book tries to answer your questions and provide you with the information you need to work with your vendors. It also attempts to guide you through the months of planning that await you.

Weddings, although one of life's most traditional events, have changed over the past several years. And this book has changed, too. There is still some focus on traditional wedding ceremonies and receptions, but it keeps you current with the latest trends and new ideas. It emphasizes using your uniqueness to its fullest to make this wedding yours. Personalize is the buzzword in weddings now. With a little help from this book, you will be able to glide through this process without much friction.

This book is the result of the experience and pleasure I have gained in helping more than 425 couples enjoy the wedding of their dreams. In 1985, I began my wedding consulting business, Bearable Weddings by Teddy. In the ensuing 22 years, I have shared ideas and learned from countless other wedding professionals through seminars and conferences. I have learned the hard way how to choose competent and professional vendors and how to avoid potential nightmares. I have also broadened my horizons through the give-and-take of teaching a noncredit course, "How to Plan and Enjoy Your Wedding," for Indiana State University in Terre Haute, Indiana.

I've always been a believer in continuing education, and in 1993, I obtained the highest level of recognition the Association of Bridal Consultants awards: Master Bridal Consultant™. It took me 7 years to achieve that, but my learning never stops. I learn so much from the brides and grooms I've had the pleasure of working with—that alone could fill a book.

I've been where you are right now about 425 times. I know the frustration you're feeling, the intimidation, and the feelings of being overwhelmed at the same time that you're so happy you could just burst.

Well, slow down. Take a deep breath and get ready for some major work on understanding the wedding industry. That knowledge will help you gain an insight into a field you probably know nothing about. Once you have some understanding and knowledge of the wedding industry, you'll be better equipped to be an intelligent wedding consumer. That's the name of the game.

Become an intelligent wedding consumer, and spend your dollars wisely. Understand your responsibilities, and figure out the best way to approach them. Most of all, enjoy! This should be one of the most pleasant, fun-filled, exciting times in a couple's life. This book can help with that. It won't make the process of planning perfect, but it can help take the bumps out of the road to a very bearable—and wonderful!—wedding.

How to Use This Book

In these pages, you—the bride and groom—will learn what can help make your life and the lives of your family and friends so much easier as you plan for the big day. It's really not difficult, but it will require some time and energy on your part. The sole purpose of this book is to take the overwhelmingly complicated task of planning a wedding and make it E-A-S-Y.

Before you spend a dime, I suggest that you read this book from cover to cover. Try not to get so carried away with the romance and the newness of being engaged that you lose your sense of perspective. Use a highlighter to mark the points you need to understand more fully. Take notes on possible vendors you want to contact. Really use this book! Its unique design will give you all the help you need. The more you use it, the easier your planning will be. Do not rush right out and reserve a catering hall, for example, before you read this book. Let me help you determine what to look for in a facility that's going to be a big part of your wedding day and your wedding dollars.

Here's how this book is organized:

Part 1, "Don't Spend a Dime Yet!" gets you off on the right foot. Here I talk about understanding the

ever-growing wedding industry and how to get started on this wonderful adventure of planning your wedding. I share some tips on finding a good bridal consultant. I tell you about the different formalities of weddings and how to determine which fits your ideas and needs so you can decide on a realistic budget for your big day.

In **Part 2, "First Things First,"** I tell you how to find the right ceremony site and what choices are available. I also discuss the types of reception facilities available and those that will be part of your overall budget. I also cover your wedding party—who to ask, what to dress them in, etc. A part of the planning that often gets left to last is planning the rehearsal dinner; I'll cover that, too.

Part 3, "Putting It All Together," covers lots and lots of planning ideas. I go into detail about the reception menu and your liquor responsibilities, how to find the right florist for your taste, and information on choosing the music for both the ceremony and reception. I devote a chapter to finding that perfect gown and tux and also discuss the wide variety of transportation ideas that are available now. I also share tips on finding and working with a photographer and videographer. And I round out this part with chapters on reception agenda, invitations, favors, and budget-saving ideas.

In **Part 4, "Circling the Wagons: Preparing for the Main Event,"** I talk about the wedding stress that accompanies most wedding-planning processes and give you tips on what you can do to help yourself stay sane. I talk about divorced parents, the "control" issue, and ways to get help if you need it. And I finally touch on prenuptial preparations and that long walk down the aisle.

Part 5, "Extra Special Weddings," covers about different kinds of "special" weddings, like theme weddings or weddings that surround a certain holiday. I also talk about a newer trend, the destination wedding.

In Appendix A, you'll find worksheets to make it easier to choose and work with major vendors. For example, the "Photography" Worksheet gives you plenty of space to fill in the information you need to keep on file for your records. I hope you'll use these worksheets, as they'll help you stay organized.

Finally, Appendix B offers a planning checklist to help you keep track of all the details in the months leading up to the wedding.

Extras

To help you get the most out of this book, I've added the following special information boxes scattered throughout:

Nuptial Notes

Check these sidebars for simple definitions of wedding terminology.

Wedding Woes

Check these sidebars for cautions about possible pitfalls and solutions to common problems you might encounter.

Bouquet Toss

In these sidebars, I share wedding trivia and stories of other couples.

Teddy's Tips

In these sidebars, I offer expert tips that can help you be more efficient or save you money.

Acknowledgments

I cannot believe this is the fifth edition! And a totally new version at that. The hundreds of photographs featured in this new illustrated edition are wonderful additions! I am humbled that I was asked to write the first edition, and now, four editions later, the fifth one is about to make its debut. My thanks to Alpha for having the confidence and trust in me to write another edition. To my editor, Randy Ladenheim-Gil, your support, humor, patience, and understanding have meant a great deal to me. It has been a sincere pleasure to work with you again. Thank you very much, my friend. To Christy Wagner, my development editor, a huge thank you, too. Your humor adds to the mix of sanity. And to all the other "behind-the-scenes folks" at Alpha, thank you. You are the ones who make my job easy.

Because of the many photographs in this edition, I owe a huge thank you to all the wonderful photographers and bridal consultants who lent me their fantastic images. These are some of the most outstanding photographers in the country. They cover weddings from coast to coast. A big thanks to Michael Colter of Colter Photography in Indianapolis, Indiana. Michael was my mainstay, providing photos and spending hours upon hours with me trying to find that "perfect" picture. No matter where our paths take us, I will always be indebted to him. If you find one of these photographers or consultants in your area and decide to use them for your wedding, please tell them where you saw their work and read their name.

These fantastic photographers and consultants include the following:

Colter Photography—Michael Colter
Indianapolis, Indiana
317-465-9744
www.colterphotography.com

Wyant Photography, Inc.—Jim and Lois Wyant
Zionsville, Indiana
317-873-2282
www.wyantphoto.com

Broadway Photography, LLC—Kymberly Henson and Jay Bachemin
Cincinnati, Ohio
513-621-1595
www.broadwayphotoandvideo.com

Garbo Productions—Margaret Busk
Chicago, Illinois
773-477-4210
www.garboproductions.com

Frank Event Design—Frank Andonoplas, MBC™
Chicago, Illinois
773-275-6804
www.frankeventdesign.com

The Wedding Casa—Norma Edelman
San Diego, California
619-298-9344
www.weddingcasa.com

Aisle of View—Merry Beth Turpin
Kirkland, Washington
425-427-2277
www.aisleofview.com

Tony Campbell, Photojournalist
Indiana State University
812-237-3788
www.indstate.edu

Orange Enterprise, Inc.—Association of Wedding Gown Specialists
Orange, Connecticut
1-800-501-5005
www.WeddingGownSpecialists.com

Davis Jewelers
Louisville, Kentucky
502-212-0420
www.davisjewelers.com

Photography by Monique Feil
San Diego, California
619-583-1150
www.moniquefeil.com

Wedding Day Art—Lin Eagle
and Sonia Stein
Chicago, Illinois
773-267-1488 or 630-834-0482
www.weddingdayart.com

Randy Bick Photography, Inc.
Lakeside Park, Kentucky
859-341-5278
www.randybick.com

Fairy Godmothers Weddings
and Events—Beth Torstrick
Louisville, Kentucky
502-558-6061
www.fairygodmothersevents.
com

Craig Paul Studio—
Craig Tomeny
Louisville, Kentucky
502-254-7894
www.craigpaulstudio.com

Brad Baskin Photography
Chicago, Illinois
312-733-2192
www.lifetime-weddings.com

Melanie Mauer Photography
Lexington, Kentucky
859-552-3686
www.melaniemauer.com

Darwin's Photography, Inc.—
Darwin Lloyd and Reggie Lloyd
Louisville, Kentucky
502-451-8886
www.darwinsphotography.com

Emily's Images—
Emily Gruenert
Terre Haute, Indiana
812-238-9242

One Fine Day Wedding
Consultation—
Mackenzie Spalding
Lexington, Kentucky
859-536-6229
www.OneFineDayKY.com

Northern Lights
Photography—Eric Sartoris
Seattle, Washington
206-284-8495
www.weddingphotos.com

Renaissance Photography
by r.d. hunt
Indianapolis, Indiana
317-691-7484
www.RenaissancePhotography.
com

FOTOBRICENO—
Juan Carlos Briceno
Alexandria, Virginia
703-299-0009
www.FOTOBriceno.com

Troy Hill Photography, LLC
Indianapolis, Indiana
317-431-7400
www.troyphoto.com

Kay Krober Invitations &
Celebrations
Carmel, Indiana
317-733-9570
www.kaykrober.com

Gloria Boyden, ABC™
Carmel, Indiana
317-566-8233

Elegant Events by Elisa, LLC—
Elisa MacKensie, CSEP
Covington, Kentucky
859-261-3262
www.elegant-events.com

Beautiful Occasions—
Lois Pearce, MBC™
Hamden, Connecticut
203-248-2661
www.beautifuloccasions.com

Trademarks

All terms mentioned in this book that are known to be or are suspected of being trademarks or service marks have been appropriately capitalized. Alpha Books and Penguin Group (USA) Inc. cannot attest to the accuracy of this information. Use of a term in this book should not be regarded as affecting the validity of any trademark or service mark.

Accredited and Master Bridal Consultant are trademarks of the Association of Bridal Consultants.

PART 1

Don't Spend a Dime Yet!

IN THIS PART

1 Taking Your First Steps Toward the Altar
2 Simple or Extravagant? Setting Your Budget

Y ou're engaged to a wonderful person. You've been on cloud nine since the proposal. You've announced the good news to your family and friends, and now you can't wait to get started on the wedding plans. Planning a wedding is a big deal, and the wedding business is big business. The more you know about the industry and how to use it to your advantage, the better your planning will be and the more relaxed you'll be when you finally walk down that aisle.

So catch your breath, let your feet touch down for a moment, and ready yourself to read Part 1. Here I introduce you to some of the things you should know before you write that first check. You'll find advice on how to start your planning, which questions to ask, and where to go for help. You'll learn how to determine the type of wedding you want to have and how that decision can affect your wedding budget.

CHAPTER 1

Taking Your First Steps
Toward the Altar

IN THIS CHAPTER

- Big business: understanding the wedding industry
- Getting organized
- Checking out bridal shows
- Should you work with a bridal consultant?
- Logging on to the best wedding websites

You wouldn't go out and buy the first car you saw without doing some research on its qualities or gas mileage; you might even consult *Consumer Reports* for expert tips. Likewise, you wouldn't have any kind of surgery without first consulting and interviewing several doctors. And you wouldn't go looking for the perfect home without the help of a reputable real-estate agent. The same is true for the wedding industry. You need to understand what's out there and what's available before you start spending your precious dollars.

Before you make that first purchase, you need to understand what the wedding industry is all about and how to get organized. In this chapter, you'll also find the best online resources to help you along your path to wedding bliss.

Understanding the Wedding Industry

The first thing you need to know about weddings in the United States is that the wedding industry is big business. In 2005, the most recent figures available, the wedding industry grossed between $72 and $106 *billion*, second only to the holiday season in retail! That figure doesn't cover just the wedding itself. It also covers the rings, the honeymoon, and setting up your new home.

Understanding how big the industry is might give you some perspective on why you don't want to rush right out and reserve the first reception site you see. The wedding process will cost you some money, but you don't have to break the bank to have the wedding of your dreams—if you plan wisely. (I'll tell you how to set up a budget you can live with in Chapter 2.)

He's slowly slipping on the ring. What an exciting moment!

(PHOTO BY COLTER PHOTOGRAPHY)

An engagement photo can be taken almost anywhere. This couple seems to be enjoying one of their favorite spots.

(PHOTO BY FOTOBRICENO)

Finding an Organizational System

The number-one suggestion I make to brides is to use some kind of organizational system. It doesn't matter whether it's a three-ring binder, a CD-ROM program, or a folder with pockets. (Obviously, this book will be a big part of your system!) Keep everything that relates to your wedding in this planner: receipts, contracts, material swatches, a calendar with appointments marked, phone numbers of vendors, and reminder lists. Be sure you have this planner with you whenever you visit a vendor. If you are organized, you will be able to enjoy the whole planning process so much more.

Bridal Shows

You've figured out a system you're comfortable with and one you'll use. Now what? Depending on how much time you have, you might want to attend a bridal show in your area. Bridal shows are great ways to meet the vendors from your area whose services you'll be using. The usual format for such events might include time to talk with individual vendors, a fashion show by area bridal shops, and sometimes drawings for door prizes the vendors provide.

What to Expect

The whole idea behind bridal shows is twofold: you get to see what's available in your area, and the vendor gets your name and address for possible contact. The bride and groom, or the parents of a bride or groom, can browse the different vendors—jewelers, caterers, florists, and photographers, to name a few—and get a feel for what they have to offer.

Getting the Most from a Bridal Show

Brides who get the most from these shows talk to the folks behind the booth tables and listen to what they have to say. When you're at a bridal show, speaking with vendors, keep the following in mind:

- Is it hard-sell approach?
- Does the product look like something you would want at your wedding?
- Do they have handouts and brochures for you to peruse at your leisure?

Wedding Woes

Watch for professional behavior from vendors: appearance, mannerisms (gum chewing—yuck!), good grammar, eye contact, and so on. How do they present themselves? If they act bored or uninterested when you speak with them, how much effort and enthusiasm are they likely to put into your wedding?

Mom and bride discuss favors with this consultant at the Art of the Table bridal show. There are all kinds of ideas here, just for the asking.

(PHOTO BY COLTER PHOTOGRAPHY)

The Role of the Bridal Consultant

Working one on one with the bride and her family from the engagement to the honeymoon, or any points in between, the *bridal consultant* can ensure that all aspects of your wonderful day happen as you had planned. Some couples hire consultants as soon as they announce their engagement. I've actually had mothers call me for advice and counsel before their daughters even have a ring, much less have a date chosen. Other couples choose to hire a consultant near the end of the process—6 weeks or so from the actual wedding day—to pull together those loose ends and to oversee the rehearsal and wedding day activities. The bottom line here is that you should decide just how much you want to involve the bridal consultant. You're the boss; the final choice should always be yours.

𝒩uptial 𝒩otes

A **bridal consultant** works directly with the bride and groom, or the couple's parents, to help facilitate the wedding. Most bridal consultants have independently owned businesses. Their expertise is in finding the right vendors to meet your budgetary needs and keeping you on track with your checklist as you count down the days until your wedding. The bridal consultant is there to help you have your dream wedding at the best possible price.

Finding the Right Consultant for Your Wedding

Where do you find a bridal consultant? You can look in the Yellow Pages as a first step, as long as you review the listings carefully. The best method, however, is to ask friends and family for names of consultants they've worked with. Many vendors will also recommend area bridal consultants they have worked with and whom they feel comfortable with. In addition, the church may have worked with bridal consultants they felt especially good about having at the wedding.

When comparing bridal consultants, look for one who is a member of an organization of wedding professionals. This generally indicates that the consultant is continually learning, attending conferences to further her knowledge, and keeping aware of changes and trends in the wedding industry.

And you should always ask the bridal consultant for references. See the "Bridal Consultant Worksheet" in Appendix A for more information.

Bouquet Toss

There are no "wedding police." If you truly want to do something at your wedding or during the planning stages that may not be proper etiquette, get some impartial advice. Try to determine whether the custom truly is not in good taste or whether it simply isn't a commonly practiced custom.

The Association of Bridal Consultants

You can also get the names of consultants in your area by contacting certain trade associations, such as the Association of Bridal Consultants (ABC). The ABC is the largest organization for bridal consultants in the world. In 1982, ABC had just 2 members worldwide; as of April 2006, it has a worldwide membership of more than 4,800 members, and that number climbs higher each year.

The ABC will be happy to give you names of members in your area. Call (1-860-355-0464), fax (1-860-354-1404), or e-mail (office@bridalassn.com) for more information.

Using the Internet: Show Me Your Sites!

With the exponential growth of all things Internet recently, you have the world of wedding planning and shopping at your fingertips—literally! Take advantage of the ease of online shopping or just browsing to help you get ideas or even find vendors and other wedding goodies.

The Internet has grown so much since I last updated this book in 2004 that the changes are hard to keep up with! The websites you can choose from are endless, and the mass of information can boggle the mind. As of this writing, all the websites listed here are active and well established.

Personal Bridal Pages

A recent trend is for brides and grooms to have a web page all about them and their wedding. And why not? Everything else seems to be online now, as you'll see in the following sections.

Should you have a web page? The answer is *yes!* It will save you time and money and help you communicate better with your family and friends. Imagine your page with a picture of the two of you and a little background information. A brief synopsis of your jobs, hobbies, and heritage will help friends and family get better acquainted with you. Post your wedding date, time, location, and reception information, and include a map (a must for out-of-town guests) so all your essential information is in one easy place.

Also include on your web page where you're registered for gifts. Many national chain stores are online and linked with their stores all over the world. Two websites that allow you to set up your own personal web page for your wedding free of charge are the following:

- www.theknot.com
- www.weddingdetails.com

These two sites also offer wedding advice via e-mail.

Bridal Shows

Here are some websites that feature wedding shows:

- www.bridal-shows.com
- www.bridalfashionshows.com
- www.bspishows.com

Bridal Consultants

The ABC has made it easy to find a consultant in your area: you e-mail a request, and they locate a consultant near you and send you his or her information.

Check these sites for more information:

- www.afwpi.com
- www.bridalassn.com

Wedding Portals/Directories

Wedding portals/directories are the easiest way to find information on weddings. A portal is like a mall, but everyone in the "mall" is in the same type of business—it's one-stop shopping for weddings.

Caterers, bridal shops, coordinators, clergy, and so on from your area are all located in the same place. This enables you to stop searching the web and start concentrating on viewing products and contacting professionals.

Click over to these must-see sites:

- www.theknot.com
- www.weddingchannel.com
- www.weddingdetails.com
- www.weddingnetwork.com

Wedding Stores Online

Several online stores contain thousands of products, from favors to centerpieces and everything in between. Check out these sites for a multitude of ideas, products, and options to fit your budget and taste. When you've decided on your wedding theme and colors, it'll be very easy to visit these online stores and order without having to drive around the state. Sites to see include the following:

- www.modernbride.com
- www.theweddingshopper.com
- www.weddingdetails.com

Online Bridal Registries

It's never been easier to register online. With thousands of items to choose from and all those extra ones you want to register for, you can't miss. Online registry offers you the convenience of registering where you like without having to worry about whether or not a certain store is in your area. Perhaps you would like to add a glass vase from Macy's in New York to your list, but most of your friends and family live in Idaho. Online registry is the answer, enabling friends to order conveniently and safely over the Internet. Check out these registry sites:

- www.a-weddingday.com
- www.giftpoint.com
- www.theweddingshopper.com
- www.weddingnetwork.com

Wedding Planning Sites

These websites offer links to all areas of planning, from consultants to florists to photographers:

- www.theknot.com
- www.weddingchannel.com
- www.weddingdetails.com

Destination Weddings

As you'll learn in Chapter 19, a *destination wedding* is a wedding you plan from one area and all your guests travel to the wedding. It's usually held in a vacation location such as Disney World, Hawaii, or someplace equally special.

These sites offer help with planning a wedding in another location:

- www.unforgettablehoneymoon.com
- www.weddinglocation.com

Wedding Traditions

Weddings that call for unusual special effects or costumes to carry out the wedding theme can be fun, fun, fun, as you'll see in Chapter 18! For a fun themed wedding, visit the following websites:

- www.medieval-weddings.net
- www.weddingdetails.com/lore

Tuxedos

Refer your groom-to-be and his groomsmen to the following sites for information on tuxedoes:

- www.afterhours.com
- www.fubu.com
- www.tuxedos.com

THE LEAST YOU NEED TO KNOW

- Use a system of organization—a CD-ROM program, a notebook, or a folder—to hold your receipts, brochures, fabric swatches, vendor phone numbers, appointment calendar, and so on.
- Attending a bridal show can be a good way of learning about wedding vendors and comparing prices and services.
- Working with a bridal consultant can help you be sure all the aspects of your big day go as planned.
- Check out the Internet for information regarding anything and everything to do with your wedding.

(PHOTO BY MELANIE MAUER PHOTOGRAPHY)

CHAPTER 2

Simple or Extravagant?
Setting Your Budget

IN THIS CHAPTER

- Deciding how formal you want your wedding to be
- Understanding how the level of formality affects your budget
- Setting a budget you can realistically work with
- Determining whom to involve with the finances

In this chapter, I cover the financial part of the wedding. *Ugh!* you may be thinking. I know, it's not a popular topic, but it's necessary. Without a realistic budget in mind, you'll be overspending long before you know it.

Before you set a budget, though, you need to understand several factors to make your wedding dollars count. The first question to ask yourself is how formal you and your partner want your wedding to be. Have you always dreamed of a large formal church wedding, or is a relaxed outdoor wedding with just family

and a few close friends more your style? And you'll want to discuss what important elements of the wedding and reception you and your groom want included. Sit down with each other and go over the "What's Important to Us Worksheet" in Appendix A. Prioritize your ideas so you know how you want to divide your precious wedding dollars. If wonderful photography is high on your list, for example, make a note of that so when it comes time to divide the overall budget, you'll know that's one area in which you want to allocate more money.

This couple is dressed in all white. The groom is wearing a new-look tux with a long white tie. The bride is wearing a gown featuring arm treatments for some interesting accents.

(PHOTO BY GARBO PRODUCTIONS)

Blue Jeans or Black Tie?

Determining how formal you want your wedding to be will help you establish the basis for your overall wedding strategy. The level of formality you choose determines, to a great extent, the overall cost of your wedding. It's a good idea for all participants—the bride, the groom, the in-laws, and anyone else with a financial interest in this wedding—to sit down together and figure out just how detailed and formal you want this affair to be. Essentially, you can choose from the following four levels of formality:

- Ultraformal
- Formal
- Semiformal
- Informal

Ultraformal: Glamorous and Glitzy

The most formal type of wedding you can have is *ultraformal*. This is the kind of wedding a movie star, royalty, or the president's daughter might have. Of course, you can have this type, too, and it doesn't necessarily mean you have to have it in a large church. Ultraformal weddings usually include the following:

- Usually more than 500 guests.
- A large wedding party—9 to 15+ bridesmaids and groomsmen.
- Elaborate decorations and floral arrangements.
- A variety of music selections both at the ceremony and reception.
- A formal served dinner.
- Place cards and menu cards at the reception tables.
- Formal programs for both the ceremony and reception.
- A detailed bride's gown, with beading and pearls. (The bride might also have a separate gown for the reception.) The bridal gown is always full length with, most times, a cathedral-length train (the longest type).
- A veil (either short or full length).
- If the reception is after 6 P.M., the groom and his groomsmen should be in white tie and tails. If the reception is before 6 P.M., formal black tie is the attire.
- A full bar at the reception.
- Favors for the guests.
- Formalwear for the guests, with men in tuxedos and women in long gowns.

This pretty bride wears a formal gown with capped, off-the-shoulder sleeves, beaded bodice, and a full veil.

(PHOTO BY BROADWAY PHOTOGRAPHY)

A large factor in determining how formal your wedding will be is deciding how many guests you want to invite. Start with a number you can comfortably entertain at the reception, and divide that number by 4. This process can vary depending on your personal family situation, but normally the bride's parents, the groom's parents, the bride, and the groom all submit guest lists. There may be duplicates on the lists, so check for that.

This is an example of a mantia veil made with heavier lace. Usually a mantia doesn't have a "blusher" or veil covering the face, but this one does.

(PHOTO BY FOTOBRICENO)

This couple is formally dressed with the groom in black tux with white bow tie and the bride in a halter-top gown with ruffles down the train and skirt of the gown. She is wearing a cathedral-length veil.

(PHOTO BY GARBO PRODUCTIONS)

Formal: Elegant and Graceful

The *formal* wedding currently is the most popular type of wedding in most parts of the United States. A formal wedding normally includes the following:

- 150 to 350 guests.
- 3 to 8 bridesmaids and groomsmen.
- Either a seated dinner, heavy hors d'oeuvres, or grazing stations.
- A full or limited bar.
- Several musical groups for the ceremony and reception.
- Brides' gowns can be elaborate or more simple, to suit the bride, but they should still be full length with either a chapel- or cathedral-length train.

- A veil (either short or full length).
- Men in the wedding party wear tuxedos.

- Favors are usually given to the guests.
- Guests wear suits and ties for the men and cocktail dresses or suits for the ladies.

Semiformal: Tasteful and Dignified

The *semiformal* wedding generally includes the following:

- 100 to 200 guests.
- 1 to 4 bridesmaids and groomsmen.
- The bride is dressed more simply. She might wear flowers or a comb in her hair instead of a veil

Wedding Woes
Weddings tend to grow in size and complexity. Think carefully now about your options and what you want to include. As you start adding to your must-have list, the complexity and costs can easily begin snowballing!

This bride chose to wear gloves with her gown, while her groom chose a traditional tux with bow tie.
(PHOTO BY MELANIE MAUER PHOTOGRAPHY)

- Men in wedding party may not wear tuxedos.
- The reception might consists of hors d'oeuvres and a limited bar.

- Decorations are simpler.
- A disc jockey or small combo may provide the music.

This groom chose the new tailored tuxedo with a long tie. It looks more like a suit.

(PHOTO BY RAAB)

The bride chose a strapless gown with bugle beads and re-embroidered lace on the bodice. Her veil features bugle beading along the edge.

(PHOTO BY RAAB)

Informal: Casual and Comfortable

An *informal* wedding is usually conducted either in a judge's chambers, in a home setting, or outdoors. Most times, an informal wedding includes the following:

- Fewer than 50 guests.
- Just one honor attendant each.
- Simple food, such as cake and punch or champagne for the toast.

- Simple décor, such as one floral arrangement, with the bride carrying a simple bouquet.
- Both bride and groom wear simple suits, or the bride may opt for a street-length wedding dress.
- The couple may choose to have a larger party later to celebrate their marriage with family and friends.

How the Level of Formality Affects Your Budget

The type of wedding you decide to have—ultraformal, formal, semiformal, or informal—plays a huge part in determining the overall cost of your wedding. The standards that determine the level of formality, however, are not carved in stone, and there are no hard-and-fast rules. Your wedding may cross over into a couple formality levels, but you do need a starting point. Choose the level of formality you are most comfortable with and seems to fit best within your budget.

Setting a Realistic Budget

The *wedding budget* is probably the biggest area of turmoil for most couples. No one—I repeat, no one—wants to talk about the cost of the wedding. But ultimately, you do have to broach the subject, and the earlier you begin talking about it, the better.

Cost Comparison

Turn to Appendix A and glance at the "Cost Comparison Worksheet," which lists all possible wedding expenses. This worksheet helps you find the norm for your market area and determine what sets each estimate apart. It won't help you one bit if I quote you the cost of hiring a photographer in Indianapolis if you live in Boston. You have some homework to do here, but it will pay off—literally—in the end.

Now is the time to begin reviewing those names of possible vendors you've gathered from bridal shows, your family, your friends, and maybe your bridal consultant. Call at least three vendors in each category to determine where their prices fall and then record the information on this worksheet. Be sure you ask each vendor the same questions so you can compare "apples to apples."

Putting Your Budget on Paper

When you've finished the "Cost Comparison Worksheet," turn to the "Wedding Budget Worksheet," also in Appendix A. Using your completed "Cost Comparison Worksheet," run down the list of service providers.

Continue to do the same with each entry on the budget worksheet and then add up everything to see what ballpark you're in. You may be way, way out of the park, or you could be right on target.

The next step is compromise. Unless you have unlimited resources or Uncle Ralph died and left you a huge inheritance, you have to be cost-conscious in your wedding planning. If you're set on having that

Nuptial Notes

A **wedding budget** is what you can realistically expect to spend on the wedding and reception. It includes an estimate of all your other wedding expenses.

Teddy's Tips

The average cost of a formal wedding in the United States—including a dinner and bar for 200, engagement and wedding rings, a gown, menswear, a band, a photographer, a florist, invitations, bridal consultant, and all the extras—varies depending in what area of the country you live. The latest figures from *Modern Bride* magazine survey indicate that the average cost of a wedding is $26,500.

This pretty gown of ivory lace with a darker ivory ribbon belt and a silver clasp makes a nice statement. The bride carries a small nosegay of spring flowers.

(PHOTO BY CRAIG PAUL STUDIO)

top-rated photographer in your area who costs $5,000 just to book, think about ways to decrease your flower bill, or go with a DJ rather than a band. Give and take—that's the name of the game.

Getting Everyone Involved

When determining your wedding budget, be sure to include all members of the wedding finance committee. That may include the bride and groom, all parents, grandparents, and others. Sit down in a relaxed atmosphere, and talk about the expenses of the wedding. Most of all, think positive and be willing to give and take.

Wedding Woes

Never leave key players out of the budget discussion. If you don't have the financial resources to spring for this wedding on your own, you need backing from family. Play it smart

The more open you are to compromising with your budget, the less stress over money matters you're likely to have later. You're also less likely to be disappointed because your budget can't accommodate your dreams.

Who Pays for What?

Weddings are considered traditional ceremonies of a life passage. As customs and traditions have changed during the years, so have the rules for who pays for what. Traditionally, the bride's family has paid for the majority of the wedding costs. However, that's changing, and more couples are coming up with creative ways to meet their financial obligations. Today, it's not uncommon for the couple to pay all their expenses or for a combination of contributors—including both sets of parents, grandparents, and even close friends—to give funds for the wedding.

The "Who Pays for What? Worksheet" in Appendix A gives you an idea of the traditional items in a wedding budget. But this worksheet is only a guide. This is the twenty-first century, and there are many ways to divide wedding expenses. Find the way that works best for you.

This beautiful bride concentrates as she prepares for her wedding. Notice all the jewels, as is her custom.

(PHOTO BY CRAIG PAUL STUDIO)

THE LEAST YOU NEED TO KNOW

- Determining early on what level of formality you want your wedding to be lets you decide what's important. It also enables you to establish a realistic budget.

- There are no hard-and-fast rules concerning the levels of formality. What I've given here are suggestions. Find a starting point, even if the wedding you want seems to cross a couple formality levels.

- Use cost comparison to determine prices in your area. You can't begin putting together a budget if you don't have an idea of the going rate for services in your area.

- Sit down in a relaxed atmosphere with everyone who needs to be involved with the wedding finances. Be realistic in what you want and what you can afford. When you've established your budget, do your best to work within it.

- Think positive, and be willing to give and take!

PART 2

First Things First

IN THIS PART

3 Get Me a Church on Time!

4 Seeking Your Soirée

5 The Wedding Party: A Circle of Friends

6 Cast Party: Arranging the Rehearsal Dinner

In Part 2, I cover what you need to reserve first and how far before the big day you need to make the reservations. Although it might not seem like it now, there's a method to all this madness. Part 2 covers topics such as reserving the reception and the church or ceremony site. I talk about asking friends to be part of this wonderful day, discuss your wedding party, and finish up with talking about the rehearsal dinner.

Be patient. We're just getting started. The big day will be here before you know it—and you'll be ready!

(Photo by Emily's Images)

CHAPTER 3

Get Me a Church on Time!

IN THIS CHAPTER

- What to consider when choosing a date
- Finding a ceremony site
- Working well with your officiant
- Customizing your service
- Getting through—and enjoying!—the ceremony
- Receiving your guests

Some of the most obvious duties to cover at the beginning of your wedding planning are what I fondly call the "biggies": setting a date, finding a place, making the arrangements for someone to perform the service, deciding on what type of service you want to have, and customizing your service. That's not to mention the ceremony itself and how to receive your guests. You have a lot to think about!

These tasks are not as time-consuming as meeting with the caterer or visiting the reception facility, but they need to be done first. After all, if you don't have a date, how can you plan anything else?

Setting the Date

When choosing a date for your wedding, keep in mind holidays, how far guests have to travel, special events and tourist activities taking place in the area, and likely weather conditions.

This beautiful bride and groom decided to hold their ceremony in a college administration building.

(PHOTO BY THE WEDDING CASA)

This Jewish ceremony is taking place in a simple, parklike setting.

(PHOTO BY GARBO PRODUCTIONS)

Planning Around Big Events

Try your best to avoid scheduling your wedding at the same time as a popular special event.

Also check with the local convention and visitors' bureau to be sure no really big conventions are in town that will take up many hotel rooms and reception sites.

Teddy's Tips

Set your date with the church and the reception site as early as possible. Sometimes you have to juggle the date to coordinate both facilities.

Teddy's Tips

One simple thing that can easily sneak up on you is remembering to apply for the marriage license. Each state has different requirements and policies, including the length of the waiting period, the ages of both parties, blood tests (or other medical examinations), identification requirements, and the cost of the license. And within each state, each county may have its own set of rules. Call the office of the marriage clerk or county clerk in your county seat and ask how to proceed. Investigate the requirements several months before your wedding date. Many counties now make allowances for long-distance couples, but you should find out well in advance of your wedding day.

Holidays: Pressure Cookers or Money Savers?

Holiday weddings, especially during the Christmas season, can be stressful, given the hectic nature of the time of year, but they also can be money savers. Most facilities are already decked out for the holidays, which means you can save big bucks on decorations.

The cost savings doesn't come without a price, however. We all know the kind of stress that can accompany the holidays in everyday life; add the task of planning a wedding, and you compound that stress many times over. However, if you love Christmas and can handle the added pressure, you can save substantially on your decorating costs.

Selecting the Ceremony Site

You have a date in mind, and you've determined how formal you want your wedding to be. Now you need to find a place for the ceremony.

The place you choose for your wedding ceremony can be as unique as you and your partner. You have many options including, a church, a cathedral, a chapel, a temple, a hall, a private home, a garden or other outdoor setting, a private club, a restaurant or resort facility, or a judge's chambers.

This is a tent. When you take down all the fabric and lights, you're left with a white tent. Amazing!
(PHOTO BY GARBO PRODUCTIONS)

Some couples have expressed their personalities by choosing unique venues for their ceremony:

- On a hot-air balloon
- Underwater
- On a roller coaster
- On horseback
- On a beach
- In a barn or on a ranch
- On a boat

Wedding Woes

Be sure to check your state's regulations regarding marriage licenses and weddings on water! You don't want to plan your shipboard wedding only to find out it's not legal. Check with local officials first.

This is a more informal wedding. Guests are dressed even more casually, some in shorts!

(PHOTO BY NORTHERN LIGHTS PHOTOGRAPHY)

Examine the Facility Firsthand

Whether it's your home church or a rented space, be sure to visit the facility where you plan to hold your wedding ceremony. Here are some questions to ask:

- How many guests can it seat?
- What kind of musical equipment comes with it (if any)?
- What are the restrictions with the music?
- Is a room available for the bride to get dressed in, if that's necessary?
- Is parking ample and close to the facility?
- Are restroom facilities adequate?

- Does the facility have air conditioning (important if you're planning a late spring or summer wedding!)?
- Are there restrictions on vendor delivery times, such as for flowers?
- Can you bring your own clergy or officiant to perform the ceremony?
- How much time will you be allowed for the wedding? Does that include taking pictures?
- Is the room where the actual ceremony will take place large enough to accommodate your wedding party size?

This gazebo makes for an intimate setting for a ceremony.

(PHOTO BY COLTER PHOTOGRAPHY)

This dockside area is ready and waiting for the guests to arrive. Notice the red carpet, a nice touch against the sea.

(PHOTO BY THE WEDDING CASA)

This Greek Orthodox service is being held in the bridal party's church. Notice the "crowns" on the bride's and groom's heads, joined together by a ribbon. This is the part of the ceremony in which they are joined symbolically as one.

(PHOTO BY BRAD BASKER)

This outdoor setting facing the woods makes for a peaceful venue.

(PHOTO BY COLTER PHOTOGRAPHY)

Understand the Fees and Policies

Be sure to ask about fees. A church is a business, and many churches charge for the use of the facility.

Be sure to ask what the fee includes. Some churches charge a single fee that includes all the necessary services (musicians, janitor, officiant, and rent), and these are probably the best deal. You're going to have to pay for those services anyway, so if you can line them all up with one stop, that's not a bad option.

Use the "Ceremony Site Worksheet" in Appendix A to ensure that you've asked all the right questions and have thoroughly investigated a facility before you actually write the check to reserve it.

Last but certainly not least, be sure you have copies of the contract or letter of agreement (a simpler form of a contract) from the ceremony site. Don't rely on "I'll put you down for that date" from the church secretary. A written contract reserving your date with the facility is best.

Wedding Woes

Be sure you read and fully understand the church's (or other facility's) wedding policies before your wedding day. If you can't work with its rules, look elsewhere. If there are restrictions on certain parts of the church rental, be sure to inform those who will be affected, such as your vendors.

Working With the Officiant

Whether the officiant is a justice of the peace, a judge, a priest, a rabbi, or a minister, someone with the legal authority allowed by the state must preside at your marriage. My best advice when working with this person is to make him or her your friend. After all, the officiant is going to perform a very important ceremony in your life, and you want fond memories of this event.

Meet with the officiant. Ask for opinions and advice. Get him or her on your side first and then talk about the particulars of your service.

Certainly, most officiants are pleasant and friendly and want to help make your wedding day memorable. A little common respect and courtesy can go a long way toward making the officiant a friend.

This is a Jewish/Protestant service held at a Unitarian church. The couple incorporated a rabbi and a minister and had both their brothers as the "honor attendants."

(PHOTO BY COLTER PHOTOGRAPHY)

What a striking setting for a ceremony. Notice her gown: it's draped to one side—lovely!
(PHOTO BY WYANT PHOTOGRAPHY)

Customizing Your Service

You want your service to reflect your personalities and your uniqueness as a couple—but where do you start? First, before you do anything, you need to speak with the officiant about what you can do and, perhaps more important, what you *cannot* do. Some churches and officiants have strict rules about what must be included in the ceremony according that religion. If you work with the officiant, most will let you add some personal touches to make it more personal for you. After all, it is *your* wedding.

Or maybe you don't want a religious service at all. Whatever your preference, you still need to check with the officiant to see what's acceptable. If you use a judge or clerk of the court to perform the service, most times they will read from a script you provide them. But still, out of courtesy, check with the officiant first.

Heritage is a big part of some weddings. Here, a couple jumps over a broom, part of African American tradition.

(PHOTO BY GARBO PRODUCTIONS)

Writing Your Vows

One of the best ways to make the service truly a part of you is to write your own vows. After you have the go-ahead from your officiant, sit down with your fiancé. Talk about what elements are important to each of you, get some resource books, and then start writing. Your vows don't have to mirror each other's. Just speak from the heart.

This couple stands before the congregation (and all those beautiful candles) to pledge their love.

(PHOTO BY FOTOBRICENO)

Notice the placement of the minister in front of the couple so guests can see them instead of the minister's face.

(PHOTO BY WYANT PHOTOGRAPHY)

You can also personalize your service in several other ways:

- Add songs to your service, either with a soloist or choir.
- Use some different musical instruments to add a spark to the service. Some favorites are harp, strings, trumpet(s), or flute.
- Readings from either the Bible or from other sources such as Kahlil Gibran's *The Prophet* can be included.

- Make your ceremony a true candlelight ceremony. Give everyone in the congregation candles, and light them during the service. This is a beautiful way to spread your love.

Teddy's Tips

A good resource to check out is *Weddings from the Heart: Contemporary and Traditional Ceremonies for an Unforgettable Wedding* by Daphne Rose Kingma (Red Wheel/ Weiser, 1995) or *The Pocket Idiot's Guide to Wedding Vows* by Robyn S. Passante (Alpha Books, 2005).

The Ceremony! What Will Happen?

All systems are *go*. You had the rehearsal the night before. You even got a good night's sleep. You've spent the day with your bridesmaids having your hair and makeup done, and the pictures are finished! The guests are seated. Both mothers have been escorted to their seats. Your bridesmaids begin to move down the aisle. You hear the trumpet fanfare and know *this is it*.

Take a deep breath—seriously. Controlling your breathing has a calming effect on your body and mind. Relax and walk *s-l-o-w-l-y*. After all, this is one walk you want to make the most of. You want to be poised, proud, happy, and maybe even a little teary-eyed.

When you reach the altar, depending on what type of service you have, you may either leave the arm of your father (or whoever is escorting you) or stay with him until the officiant asks the famous question, "Who *brings* this woman?" (Notice we don't *give* anymore.)

Now you're in the hands of the officiant and, trust me, he (or she) has probably done this hundreds of times and likely hasn't lost a couple yet. Just take your time, wait for the officiant's lead, and try to remember every moment of this wonderful experience.

After the "You may now kiss your bride" part, you turn and, with the sound of chimes or bells and music, you head back down the aisle.

Oh, My Aching Hand!

If you decide to use a traditional receiving line, you have to determine in advance where it will be and who will participate. More and more couples are declining the formal receiving line for a less time-consuming releasing of the aisles. Still other couples just meet guests at the reception.

Wedding Woes

Most guests feel cheated if they don't personally get to say "Hi" to you, tell you how beautiful you look, and congratulate you. If you do nothing formal at either the ceremony site or the reception site, you could face a reception of interruption after interruption. Guests *want* to see you, and they will find a way.

A lot depends on the number of guests you have at the service. Greeting 400 guests takes a lot more time than greeting 100.

Here's one way to have the parents and the couple in a formal receiving line: guests enter the receiving line from the left and move to the right. If your parents are divorced and not on good speaking terms, just have the two of you stand in the line. That will be faster, too.

Another great way to greet guests at the ceremony site is for the couple to release the rows. Instead of having the ushers going back in and releasing pews, you and your new spouse can go back and, starting with the bride's parents and then the groom's parents, zigzag your way down the center aisle. For some reason, this is a much quicker way to have a "receiving line."

This handsome couple stands at the altar.

(PHOTO BY WYANT PHOTOGRAPHY)

Lighting the unity candle.

(PHOTO BY WYANT PHOTOGRAPHY)

The exchange of rings. Notice all the lovely candles on and behind the altar.

(PHOTO BY WYANT PHOTOGRAPHY)

It's all done here now. On to the reception!

(PHOTO BY FOTOBRICENO)

Taking the time to carefully plot the order of events that will occur at the ceremony site will help your day run as smoothly as possible. And it will help reduce your stress level. This is where expert advice from those professionals who deal with this on a daily basis makes sense. Even if you buy only a couple hours of time to meet with a wedding coordinator, I think you'll find it very beneficial in your planning.

Teddy's Tips

If the bride and groom go back into the ceremony site to release the guests, I usually tell the parents to not stand in one spot outside the ceremony site or you'll end up with a second receiving line. I advise them to mingle with their guests. Just don't let a line get formed.

A beautiful spot for that first meeting as husband and wife.

(PHOTO BY WYANT PHOTOGRAPHY)

THE LEAST YOU NEED TO KNOW

- Consider weather conditions and local special events and celebrations when choosing your wedding date.

- Visit the site in person to check out location, layout, the number of guests it will hold, and parking. Be sure to understand all fees and policies.

- Treat the officiant with respect. Try your best to work with him or her to ensure a smooth road both to the church and down the aisle.

- Talk with the officiant about customizing your service. Don't go overboard with the extras, but do add something to make it more personal.

- Decide what type, if any, receiving line you want prior to the ceremony.

(PHOTO BY COLTER PHOTOGRAPHY)

CHAPTER 4

Seeking Your Soirée

IN THIS CHAPTER

- Getting what you pay for in your reception facility
- Reserving the reception site
- Finding a good caterer

Okay, folks, it's time to talk about the reception—quite possibly the biggest party you will ever throw. Getting the party you want takes careful, timely planning and lots of research.

The reception can be the most costly item in your wedding budget. In addition to finding and reserving the reception site, you need to know what to look for in a good catering facility and a caterer, and you need to make the big decision: whether or not to serve liquor. So let's party on!

A hotel formal ballroom is the setting for this reception, complete with beautifully sculptured columns and striking chandeliers.

(PHOTO BY GARBO PRODUCTIONS)

The Reception Site—Getting What You Pay For

The reception (including facility rental and catering costs) accounts for about 40 percent of your total wedding bill. When planning your wedding reception, be sure you pay close attention to all the details so you get your money's worth. (Be sure to turn to the "Reception Site Worksheet" in Appendix A for help in choosing the site.) Remember to book early; the prime reception sites are reserved as far as 18 to 24 months in advance in larger cities.

Business center complex by day ...

(PHOTO BY THE WEDDING CASA)

... perfect reception site by night. How very partylike and festive!

(PHOTO BY THE WEDDING CASA)

One Size *Doesn't* Fit All

When choosing a reception site, your biggest consideration is whether the facility is large enough to accommodate the number of guests you plan on having. Here are a few questions to start with:

- Can it comfortably accommodate your guests as well as the other areas you want to include, such as dancing and a band or disc jockey?
- Is there room to introduce the wedding party?
- Is there room for a receiving line?

Dealing With the Details

Be doubly sure that you get what the facility does and does not provide *in writing*. Here are some other "little detail" questions you'll want to ask:

- Are linens included (tablecloths, table skirting, chair covers, napkins, and so on)?
- Do you have a choice of linen colors?
- Are microphones, speakers, and other equipment included?
- Is there a dance floor? Can it be moved?
- Are there ample restrooms?
- Are there considerations for guests with physical limitations?
- Is parking adequate for guests?

An apartment building lobby is the scene for this wedding reception.

(PHOTO BY GARBO PRODUCTIONS)

Most reception sites provide those items either as part of their contract or as an add-on. Know what you're getting when you pay your deposit.

Ask questions of the manager. The manager will work with you as best he can and as the facility will allow.

This college ballroom is stately and large enough to accommodate 600 guests. Notice the fabric tied between the marble columns to soften the space.

(PHOTO BY COLTER PHOTOGRAPHY)

The head table has been placed on this auditorium stage, making good use of the space. The cake table has been placed on the floor in front of the stage.

(PHOTO BY WYANT PHOTOGRAPHY)

Reserving the Reception Site

Ask friends, family members, and recently married couples where they had their reception. That's a good starting point. Also, check in the Yellow Pages (under headings such as "Banquet Facilities," "Halls and Auditoriums," and "Party Centers") for sites.

Many reception sites—such as private clubs, halls, church social halls, restaurants, and civic centers—accept early reservations. You can reserve many of the prime reception sites at least a year in advance. In larger cities, you can book some sites as much as 18 to 24 months in advance.

Fabrics have been hung in this tent and lighting has been added to highlight certain areas.

(PHOTO BY DARWIN'S PHOTOGRAPHY, INC.)

Possible reception sites include the following:

- Private clubs
- Hotels
- Catering halls
- University or college facilities
- Victorian homes or mansions
- Art museums
- Historical society buildings
- Gardens
- Parks
- Tents
- Private homes

Traffic Jam!

The traffic flow inside the reception facility is an important factor that shouldn't be overlooked. Your reception site manager should be able to make suggestions, based on past experience, for the best traffic pattern for a wedding reception at that facility. Also check floor plans.

What About Services and Restrictions?

Check with the manager about the restrictions the facility has for food and beverages. Can you bring in an *outside caterer* of your choice, or do you have to use the facility's *in-house caterer?* Or do they have a preferred caterer list you may choose from?

Look at the "Choosing the Reception Site Worksheet" in Appendix A for more help in selecting a site.

Nuptial Notes

An **outside caterer** is a person or organization not associated with the facility who comes to the facility to prepare the food. An **in-house caterer** is the person or organization responsible for that facility's food service.

Who's in Charge Here?

Try to gauge whether you'll be able to work with the reception manager. You're going to be spending a lot of time (and money) with these people, and you want it to be a pleasant experience.

You are the client, and his or her only job for that day is to make you look good. If you look good and are happy, the reception manager (and the facility) looks good!

Choosing a Caterer

After you select a reception site, the next step is to find a caterer. If the reception facility you reserved provides an in-house catering service, you probably have no choice. Most of the larger facilities such as hotels, country clubs, colleges, or universities provide in-house catering.

If you decide to hold your reception in a hall, art museum, home, church social hall, or outdoor setting, you may have to arrange for a caterer to provide the food. If the choice of caterer is up to you, shop around and find someone who can give you the food choices you want at a price you can afford.

Friends, family, and recently married couples are your best bet when discussing possible caterers. Ask the reception facility manager, too. Sometimes facilities limit which caterers may come into their facility. They may give you their preferred caterer list and ask you to choose a caterer from that list.

Be sure to check the "Catering Worksheet" in Appendix A for help on selecting a caterer. Chapter 7 also contains detailed information about caterers.

Wedding Woes

Be wary of caterers who refuse to deviate from their standard menu. Good caterers are willing to take your favorite recipes and price them for your reception. This is great if you have some foods you particularly like or are family traditions (such as Aunt Eileen's traditional Irish soda bread).

May I Serve You?

Traditional etiquette says that the only thing you must offer your guests at the wedding reception is something to eat and something to drink, so cake and punch will do the trick. Indeed, the simplest type of wedding reception is a cake-and-punch reception, with some mints and nuts thrown in for good measure, if you so desire. Anything else is icing on the cake (pardon the pun!).

You might want to move up one step and serve hors d'oeuvres and a limited bar. A limited bar means just

A clear tent lit up at night is quite an impressive site.

(PHOTO BY COLTER PHOTOGRAPHY)

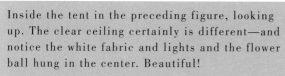

Inside the tent in the preceding figure, looking up. The clear ceiling certainly is different—and notice the white fabric and lights and the flower ball hung in the center. Beautiful!

(PHOTO BY COLTER PHOTOGRAPHY)

that: you limit the selection of liquor, perhaps opting for wine or beer and soft drinks. One step up from this would be an open bar and hors d'oeuvres. (There's more about serving liquor in Chapter 7.)

Then there's the simple buffet. This includes one entrée plus other side dishes. You can expand this into a more elaborate buffet by adding more entrées and other side dish choices.

The most elaborate reception meal you can offer would be a five- or six-course dinner, including a selection of wines with the meal.

What Will It Cost?

After you decide on the kind of meal you want to serve, start getting price estimates. Most caterers figure their prices per person, except for hors d'oeuvres, which sometimes are figured per dozen. Unless you have your heart set on particular food items, it often works well to give the caterer a price range or amount you do not want to go over and let him or her be creative. The caterer can choose the food, subject to your approval, based on seasonal availability.

Ask about the caterer's policy on guaranteed numbers. This is an important concept for you to understand before you begin contacting caterers. If you plan to serve major food items, you must have an accurate guest count. Check with the caterer about the policy on what percentage of food he or she will prepare over your guarantee; the usual is between 5 and 10 percent. So if you give the caterer a count of 100 and 105 people show up, it will be all right. If 130 show up, you're in trouble.

Be sure to build in some extra time for checking out caterers and reception sites. This is one area of wedding planning that can carry a heavy price tag, and you want to find a facility and a caterer that offer you the best value for your wedding dollars.

Lace gobo lights are projected onto the ceiling of this reception tent.

(PHOTO BY MELANIE MAUER)

Liquor: To Drink or Not To Drink?

The decision of whether to serve alcohol to your guests is solely a personal one. If you're going to offer alcohol at your reception, you need to engage either a caterer with a liquor license or a liquor-licensed dealer because of liability laws. (Direct any concerns about local laws regarding alcohol to the liquor-licensed dealer.)

Licensed bartenders are included in the contract. If the catering facility has a liquor license or if the caterer contracts the liquor to a licensed liquor dealer, it will provide the bartenders. There's usually an extra charge for bartenders, but it's well worth the cost.

Bouquet Toss

The word *bridal* comes from the old English term *bride-ale*, which refers to the mead drink (a fermented beverage made of water, honey, malt, and yeast) consumed for 30 days following the marriage.

THE LEAST YOU NEED TO KNOW

- Be sure to ask lots of questions about the physical layout of the reception site. Be sure the facility can accommodate the number of guests you're inviting. Also check whether parking is adequate.

- The reception facility should have a good traffic flow pattern. Too little room to comfortably allow for the number of guests you expect can be frustrating for everyone involved.

- Make a list of questions for the caterer before you meet with him or her. Get all details in writing of what the caterer will provide.

(PHOTO BY WYANT PHOTOGRAPHY)

CHAPTER 5

The Wedding Party:
A Circle of Friends

IN THIS CHAPTER

- Determining the size of your wedding party and who to include in it
- Having children in the wedding party
- Getting by with help from your friends

One of the best parts of planning your wedding is telling your friends the good news and asking them to share this wonderful time with you. Most people consider it an honor to be asked to be part of a dear friend or family member's wedding.

This wedding party poses for an informal shot.

(PHOTO BY RENAISSANCE PHOTOGRAPHY BY R.D. HUNT)

A water fountain makes a great background for this wedding party's photo.

(PHOTO BY GARBO PRODUCTIONS)

Because you're asking someone to stand with you on one of the most significant days of your life, be sure to put careful thought into choosing your wedding party.

Also, think about asking other friends to help with the other wedding duties, such as being the guest book attendant.

Wedding Party Size

A complaint I hear frequently is, "My groom wants to ask fourteen guys to be groomsmen. I have only eight friends for bridesmaids. Where can I get some more maids?" You don't need an even number of bridesmaids and groomsmen. Figure out exactly how many people the two of you want to stand up with you and then figure out which other jobs you can delegate to these friends.

The size of your wedding probably doesn't matter as much as your feelings for the family and friends you're about to ask to be part of one of the most wonderful days of your life.

Teddy's Tips

Talk with parents or older relatives about their wedding party. How many of the friends they "just had to have" in their wedding are they still friends with? Do they even know where some of them are today? How close are some of those "best friends"? Twenty years from now, will you look at your wedding pictures and wonder who those people are?

Pretty maids—plus one—all in a row.

(PHOTO BY NORTHERN LIGHTS PHOTOGRAPHY)

These ladies gather right before the ceremony. Beautiful colors!

(PHOTO BY WYANT PHOTOGRAPHY)

Finalizing the List

Your wedding party consists of several groups of people. The first people you ask will be the maid or matron of honor and the best man. You may refer to these people as the *honor attendants*; however, in current use, an honor attendant refers to a male maid of honor or a female best man.

The special honor of maid or matron of honor may go to a sister, a cousin, or a very close friend. You even can choose to have both a maid and a matron of honor. Both can help with some of the preliminary duties such as running errands, being a good listener, and organizing some parties.

Drinking in the scenery, these gals watch the waterfall.

(PHOTO BY NORTHERN LIGHTS PHOTOGRAPHY)

Traditionally, the bridesmaids are young women who are close to the bride such as sisters, cousins, the groom's sisters, and good friends. Bridesmaids have no official function in the wedding party but are there to be supportive.

Likewise, the groom chooses a best man. He can decide to have two best men, although this isn't as common as having both a maid and a matron of honor. The groom might even ask his father to be his best man—what an honor for a father! The best man helps the groom prepare for the wedding, making sure he arrives at the ceremony site on time. He holds the bride's ring during the service and offers the first toast to the new couple during the reception.

The groom then chooses men to serve as his groomsmen. These can be brothers, the bride's brothers, cousins, or good friends. These guys stand up with the groom and help witness the ceremony.

The remaining members of the main wedding party include the ushers, usually one usher for every 50 guests. Sometimes the groomsmen double as ushers. Other attendants making up the wedding party may include the flower girl and ring bearer, candle lighters, trainbearers, Bible bearers, junior groomsmen, junior bridesmaids, and pages. You may give these assignments to children or young adults.

Bouquet Toss

Choosing a best man keeps with the ancient custom of finding a good friend, most likely a tribal warrior, to help shield the bride from abductors known to prowl around the ceremony site.

"Let me just take a quick peep," says the bride to her little flower girl.

(PHOTO BY RENAISSANCE PHOTOGRAPHY BY R.D. HUNT)

Using Children as Attendants

Children as members of the wedding party can add joy to the day. They represent innocence and remind us of the circle of life we all share.

They also can detract more than you think from the wedding ceremony! You need to remember that children in wedding parties are still kids—they're not little adults in children's suits. They think like children, they behave like children, and they will be unpredictable like children.

The bride and her special friend.

(PHOTO BY MELANIE MAUER)

Bouquet Toss

I once coordinated a large summer wedding in which the best man and ring bearer were father and son. When I sent the flower girl and ring bearer down the aisle, as the little girl dropped the petals, the ring bearer kept reaching down and putting them back in her basket. She didn't know what to think of this pesky boy who kept messing with her petals, and he was equally frustrated that someone so cute could be so messy. Finally, he stopped halfway down the aisle and yelled to his dad, "*Daaaaaaaad*, she keeps dropping these flowers!" The father calmly answered that it was okay for her to drop the petals on the floor.

Here are some jobs you might consider assigning to special young people you want to honor:

- Ring bearer (ages 3 to 6)
- Flower girl (ages 3 to 6)
- Train bearer (ages 4 to 8)
- Guest book attendant (ages 12 and up)
- Program attendant (ages 12 and up)
- Coat checker (ages 10 and up)
- Gift attendant (ages 13 and up)
- Candle lighter (ages 10 and up)
- Altar boy or girl (Catholic service; ages 10 to 15)

These tasks are all very important and can be used to show special attention to those whom you can't include in your immediate wedding party.

Flower girls on the job.
(PHOTO BY WYANT PHOTOGRAPHY)

A kiss for good luck from the little man in the top hat (and his date!).
(PHOTO BY NORTHERN LIGHTS PHOTOGRAPHY)

Here are a couple of wedding angels, ready to float down the aisle.

(PHOTO BY THE WEDDING CASA)

Well, this ring bearer got the flower girl down the aisle—what a job!

(PHOTO BY WYANT PHOTOGRAPHY)

Other Ways to Include Friends and Family

Jobs for other adults or young people (14 and up) include the following:

- **Guest book attendant.** This person, male or female, greets guests as they enter the ceremony site or reception site and asks guests to sign the guest book.
- **Bells, petals, or bubble attendants.** These folks distribute flower petals, small bells, or small bottles of bubbles to guests as a send-off for the couple.

Wedding Woes

Traditionally, newly married couples were showered with rice, but it has been found to be harmful to the birds who later ingest it. Instead, shower couples with a more environmentally friendly alternative such as flower petals, ringing small bells, or wedding bubbles. Be aware that many facilities limit what you can toss at the new couple. Be sure to check with the facility to be sure they don't charge a cleanup fee!

- **Program attendant.** This person usually stands by the guest book and distributes the wedding programs.
- **Readers.** For both scripture and poetry.
- **Gift bearer.** During a Catholic service, the gift bearer brings the bread and wine to the priest.
- **Gift attendant.** At the reception, this person is in charge of taking gifts.
- **Reception assistants.** These folks, usually ladies, are asked to help with the reception foods, usually cutting the cake.

Two little boys being boys! I'd say they're having more fun than most of the guests.

(PHOTO BY MELANIE MAUER)

Getting a Little Help from Your Friends

Over the years, I've heard statements like these from time to time:

"Aunt Shirley is going to cater my wedding."

"My friend Ellen is doing the flowers."

"Jennifer, my sorority sister, is going to coordinate my wedding."

All these have two common elements: the couple thinks they're saving money, and they expect a professional job. They most likely will be disappointed on both counts.

There's nothing wrong with asking your friend Ellen to take care of your floral needs. She's a good friend, and you know she'll do her best. The problem comes when she doesn't—or can't—deliver what you expect. The bottom line? Don't assume that just because someone is your friend or a family member, he or she has the expertise to handle a particular task. Unless your friend or family member is a florist, photographer, or caterer by trade, it's best to leave these tasks to the professionals.

Here's a bride and her best friend. Pets are becoming more and more popular at weddings.

(PHOTO BY NORTHERN LIGHTS PHOTOGRAPHY)

THE LEAST YOU NEED TO KNOW

- Wedding party members should be those individuals you feel close to and want to include as a special part of your day.
- Use good judgment and common sense when you include children in your wedding party. Remember, children will almost always act like children. That can make for some unpredictable moments!
- There are several important tasks you can allocate to friends and family members so they're included in your wedding day.
- Be very careful when asking family and friends to do some tasks for your wedding that would be better left to the pros.

CHAPTER 6

Cast Party: Arranging the Rehearsal Dinner

IN THIS CHAPTER

- Understanding the purpose of the rehearsal dinner
- Determining who to invite
- Incorporating your own personal style
- Including all the right stuff on the agenda

The rehearsal dinner is a wedding tradition that has evolved over time. Its main purpose is to invite guests, usually family and the wedding party, to gather after the wedding rehearsal and have fun. It serves several other purposes as well, including sometimes introducing family members for the first time, letting everyone involved with the wedding ceremony have a chance to meet each other, and generally celebrating the start of the wedding festivities.

Read on to learn all you need to know about planning a rehearsal dinner, and be sure to use the "Rehearsal Dinner Worksheet" in Appendix A as a guide.

This couple is exiting their rehearsal. Now it's time to party!

(PHOTO FROM THE AUTHOR'S COLLECTION)

Why Have a Rehearsal Dinner?

You and your groom should begin thinking about a place to hold the rehearsal dinner early in the planning process. Usually, the rehearsal dinner immediately follows the wedding rehearsal, although it can be held just before the rehearsal or even on an entirely different day.

Because the rehearsal dinner is usually held the night before the ceremony, it's a good time to get friends and family members together to relax, to get to know one another, and to celebrate this wonderful occasion. In some cases, a family member or close friend might even offer to host the rehearsal dinner.

Getting to Know You

Even though the groom or his family traditionally hosts the rehearsal dinner, some planning—and conferring with the bride—is in order. It's so important for all guests to feel comfortable, so the setting for this dinner is an important factor—especially when your families come from different backgrounds. If the couple wants a very simple, casual rehearsal dinner, that should be how the event unfolds. The couple needs to understand that this is a party the groom's mother may plan, so let her have some freedom, too.

Wedding Woes

Check with all the players involved with the rehearsal dinner to be sure no one is accidentally left off the guest list. Usually, the bride's family submits a guest list to the groom's family.

A wedding around the Fourth of July calls for a picnic supper. This bride chose to use red-and-white gingham check to spruce up the tables.

(PHOTO FROM THE AUTHOR'S COLLECTION)

The silverware tied with matching ribbon adds a nice touch.

(PHOTO FROM THE AUTHOR'S COLLECTION)

The location of the rehearsal dinner is limited only by your imagination. Here are some ideas to get you thinking:

- A hotel
- A restaurant
- A beach
- A park
- A friend's home or backyard
- A boat (obviously large enough to comfortably accommodate all of your guests)
- A church social hall
- A private club
- A university or college setting

This rehearsal dinner has a more formal setting. Notice the "hot pepper" cookies as favors in this Southwest-themed dinner.

(PHOTO FROM THE AUTHOR'S COLLECTION)

Who to Invite

Your rehearsal dinner guest list might include all the key players who normally would attend the wedding rehearsal, including the following:

- The wedding party, including their spouses or dates
- Parents of the bride and groom
- Grandparents of the bride and groom
- Out-of-town family members who arrive for the wedding
- The officiant and his or her spouse
- The musicians who will be performing at the wedding and reception

- The parents of the flower girls and ring bearers (If these children are older, you may want to include them at the dinner along with their parents.)
- Soloists or readers
- Anyone else you would like to attend, within reason

If one side has more guests than the other, who makes the call on who ultimately gets to attend? Technically speaking, the person(s) hosting the rehearsal dinner make that determination, but he or she should always consult the bride and groom.

Another semi-formal table setting for a rehearsal dinner. Notice the double-fold napkins—
an easy and inexpensive way to make your tables look special.

(PHOTO FROM THE AUTHOR'S COLLECTION)

Many couples choose to send out invitations for the rehearsal dinner. As long as the invitation is not more formal than the wedding invitation, you can do what you please. Maybe a phone call inviting guests is enough for you, or maybe you've seen some wonderful informal invitations that go with the wedding theme.

Some companies also offer some great rehearsal dinner invitations.

Basically, your guest list depends on what your budget allows and the size of the facility you choose for this function. Ultimately, the choice of how large or small the guest list is, is up to the hosts.

Giving It Style

The rehearsal dinner doesn't have to be a formal, sit-down affair. Some of the more successful rehearsal dinners have been very relaxed and informal. Brides and grooms sometimes choose to have picnics, pizza parties, cookouts, or even carry-in suppers instead of a formal dinner. Remember, the primary purpose of the rehearsal dinner is to get newly merging family members together in a relaxed, informal setting.

Have It Your Way

Some couples host a themed rehearsal dinner. One couple opted for an old-fashioned, Midwestern picnic supper on their lakefront property and finished the evening with a dramatic display of fireworks.

Here are some other fun rehearsal dinner ideas:

- A riverboat rehearsal theme. (Throw in some "play" money and gamble the night away.)
- An informal night of pizza, beer, and soft drinks at home.
- A family carry-in at the church social hall.
- Hors d'oeuvres and simple cocktails at a club. (Use tall cocktail tables instead of seating guests to encourage mingling.)
- A formal dinner at a country club.
- A restaurant theme dinner. (Italian, German, Greek—celebrate your heritage.)

- A pool or beach party, complete with beach balls and a barbecue.
- Order ahead and carry-in supper from your favorite restaurant to your rehearsal site.
- An autumn theme complete with hot dogs, toasted marshmallows, a hayride, and a bonfire.

Teddy's Tips

Unless you have a tight rehearsal dinner budget, out-of-town family—especially close family members such as aunts and uncles—should be invited to the rehearsal dinner.

What's on the Agenda?

Several points need to be made during the evening at your rehearsal dinner:

- First and foremost, always take time to introduce your guests. The bride can introduce her side and the groom his and get the ball rolling with introductions.
- Thank your parents, family, and friends for their love, encouragement, and support.
- Give your wedding party their gifts.

- Take time for toasts. The father of the groom or the host offers the first toast to the bride. The second toast by the host is always to the couple. After those two toasts, the floor is open to anyone else who would like to make a toast.

Wedding Woes

The rehearsal dinner should never be more formal or more elaborate than the wedding reception.

THE LEAST YOU NEED TO KNOW

- The rehearsal dinner should be a time when family and friends—the special people in your lives—come together in a comfortable setting to meet each other and to help you launch your new life together.
- Include all members of the wedding party and their spouses or dates. It's not mandatory to invite very young children from the wedding party, but do include their parents.
- Rehearsal dinners do not have to be formal. Make it whatever you want—sit-down dinner, picnic, carry-in supper, etc. Make it a setting in which both families will feel comfortable.
- Use the rehearsal dinner as a chance to introduce everyone, say thank you, and give your gifts to the wedding party.

PART 3

Putting It All Together

IN THIS PART

7 Eat, Drink, and Be Married

8 All Dressed Up and Somewhere to Go

9 Snapdragons and Song

10 Pretty as a Picture: Photographers and Videographers

11 Extra! Extra! Read All About It!

12 Do Yourself a Favor

13 Let the Party Begin!

14 Making the Most of Your Dollars

In Part 3, you learn more about selecting the right vendor for the rest of your wedding details. I lead you on the right path for talking with caterers and understanding your liquor obligations. You learn some new ways to use flowers and what to look for in good musicians. There's a chapter on gowns—both yours and your maids—plus the men's formalwear. I talk about the reception agenda and what happens at the party of your dreams. There are invitations, favors, and programs to learn about, and finally, I show you some ways to cut costs and still have the wedding you want.

CHAPTER 7

Eat, Drink, and Be Married

IN THIS CHAPTER

- Working with the caterer and still sticking to your budget
- Deciding on what to serve
- Understanding guaranteed numbers
- Choosing a wedding cake and groom's cake
- Serving liquor—what you need to know

Regardless of how simple or elaborate you want your reception to be, menu planning takes time. I keep stressing time because the wise wedding consumer allows enough time to shop for comparisons.

In Chapter 4, I gave you some tips on choosing a caterer. Here, I cover these topics in more detail. This is a big part of your overall budget, and you can't be too careful or detailed when it comes to planning the reception. Please refer to the "Catering Worksheet" in Appendix A.

Smaller receptions let you do more interesting food displays. Notice how at this reception food is placed almost as though you were at your grandmother's home for dinner.

(PHOTO BY FOTOBRICENO PHOTOGRAPHY)

Champagne for everyone! These glasses are garnished with fresh strawberries.

(PHOTO BY BROADWAY PHOTOGRAPHY)

Working with the Caterer

When working with either an in-house or outside caterer, go to the first consultation with some notion of what kind of reception you're looking for. You should have some idea whether you're thinking a formal seated affair or food stations. Then let the caterer guide you with what works best in his or her facility.

If something you've had your heart set on is a "No" in his book, ask why. But please, ask "Why?" respectfully. You're going to be spending not only time but also money with this person, and you want to be on the best terms possible.

There's really no difference in dealing with either the in-house caterer or the outside caterer. The in-house caterer knows the property like the back of his hand,

which might be an advantage. The outside caterer has to move from reception site to reception site.

Notice how the decorator has placed individual little flowers around the base of this beautiful blue wedding cake. Also notice the words of love inscribed on the cake. A true work of art.

(PHOTO BY WEDDING DAY ART)

What's on the Menu?

After you've decided which caterer you'll be working with, choose your menu carefully. Make good use of your food choices. If you're on a limited budget for the reception (and who isn't?), be sure you thoroughly consider the time of day you choose for your wedding and reception. It has much to do with what your menu will be, etc. (Review Chapter 2 for budgeting strategies.)

Here are some reception food and beverage ideas:

- Wedding cake and punch
- Wedding cake and punch, with champagne for the toasts
- Finger sandwiches, wedding cake, and beverage
- Hors d'oeuvres and beverages

- Grazing stations and beverage stations (guests "graze" from station to station)

- Specialty food stations placed throughout the reception room offering a variety of choices (You might offer a pasta station or a seafood station, for example.)

- Buffet meal with beverages

- Plated dinner (Guests are served a preselected meal.)

Bouquet Toss

The custom of serving food at a wedding reception dates back to the ancient Greeks; they had the bride and groom share a quince (fruit). The Greeks thought that by having the couple eat this fruit, which has a bitter and sweet taste, the bride and groom were accepting the good and bad times that come with marriage. Other cultures have used the tradition of consuming food on the wedding day as a prerequisite to a good marriage. In ancient Britain, couples drank "marriage ale" for 30 days following the wedding. Those native to the South Sea Islands feasted on fruits and flowers for 30 days, after which time the couple was considered married.

This stately six-layer stacked cake looks stunning against the gold and silver linens.

(PHOTO BY RENAISSANCE PHOTOGRAPHY BY R.D. HUNT)

This interesting food display features fruits, veggies, and cheeses.

(PHOTO BY MONIQUE FEIL)

Thinking Through Your Food Options

Suppose you're going to have an hors d'oeuvres reception with a limited bar. Now you must make good use of your money as far as food selection goes. Offering liquor always means you also must serve some substantial food. You don't have to serve meat and potatoes—especially for an hors d'oeuvres reception—but you do need to provide something filling so your guests don't drink on empty stomachs.

Here are some questions to ask the caterer:

- Will the caterer prepare family recipes to serve at the reception? This is especially nice with buffets where you can place a sign that says "Aunt Emma's potato casserole."

- What add-ons are offered? Are linens included?

- What about votive candles or colored napkins?

Who could resist this great-looking—and yummy—sweets display?

(PHOTO BY MELANIE MAUER

- How much are gratuities and other service charges?

- Will the caterer prepare a "tasting" for you and your groom at the facility where you can taste the items you will serve for the reception? Some facilities will; others might charge you. It's worth it.

- Can you see photos of past receptions?

- Do they use good presentation with their food displays? Do they add greenery, flowers, and so on to make the food look inviting?

Bouquet Toss

Champagne was discovered by a monk in a northeastern region of France called Champagne. This monk found that sealing wine in a bottle for several years would cause the wine to ferment and sparkle. That monk's name was Dom Perignon. Today, Dom Perignon is one of the most well-known champagnes in the world—and a very expensive addition to your wedding reception.

This tiered cake presents a pretty picture with the bold colors used to decorate it.

(PHOTO BY THE WEDDING CASA)

Playing the Numbers Game

As I mentioned in Chapter 4, you need to talk with the caterer about what the guaranteed numbers mean. Find out what percentage the caterer will go under and above the guest count you provide. Be sure you understand how this process works.

Your guaranteed number should be an accurate count, not a guess. So many times brides say, "Oh, I know they're coming to the wedding," or, "I think we'll have about 150 people." "I think" and "I guess" are two phrases you don't want to use when it comes to guaranteeing your guest total for the caterer. This number equates to money—at times, lots of money.

Wedding Woes

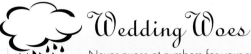

Never guess at numbers for your reception count. Guessing can destroy your food budget and leave you feeling angry, disappointed, or embarrassed. Even the best caterers cannot afford to supply your reception with unlimited amounts of food.

That Fantasy Creation: The Cake

Perhaps one of the creations given the most thought during the wedding planning stages is the wedding cake. When you're shopping for your wedding cake, be sure to ask for suggestions and recommendations from family and friends who have recently married. The caterer you're working with also might offer a wedding cake service, or he may be glad to provide you with names of competent bakers.

Notice the use of gold ribbon on this cake. Quite nicely done.

(PHOTO BY NORTHERN LIGHTS PHOTOGRAPHY)

So Many Choices …

You can select a wedding cake in a variety of flavors and fillings—another way to make a particular wedding unique. Wedding cakes today are as varied as the couples who order them. We no longer rely just on white cake. Some popular favors include the following:

- Carrot cake
- Chocolate with various fillings (Raspberry is popular.)
- Lemon
- Poppy seed with cream cheese frosting
- Red velvet
- Italian cream
- German chocolate
- Cheesecakes with a variety of toppings

This chocolate wedding cake looks too good to eat—almost!

(PHOTO BY COLTER PHOTOGRAPHY)

Bargaining with the Baker

Just as important as any vendor on your wedding list is the baker. Here are some points to consider as you make your decisions:

Ask whether the baker bakes fresh or works from frozen cakes. Some bakers bake early in the week, freeze their cakes, and decorate them on Friday, with finishing touches the day of the wedding. Get all the information; it never hurts to ask questions.

How is the cake priced? Wedding cakes usually are priced per person (meaning how many people the cake will feed). Your locale determines what that per-person charge is.

Ask whether the baker delivers the cake or whether you must arrange to pick it up. Is there an extra charge for delivery to the reception site? Most bakers deliver. They may charge for that service, but it's probably worth it.

This white iced cake features pearls and bold orange flowers.

(PHOTO BY MELANIE MAUER)

This beautiful stacked cake has a ribbon effect in the icing trailing down the side. Clusters of flowers accent it, as does the linen.

(PHOTO BY COLTER PHOTOGRAPHY)

Bouquet Toss

The first wedding cake goes back to ancient times, when the cake was actually a mixture of sesame seed meal and honey. Then, as Western Europe developed, the cake consisted of a small, unleavened biscuit. In the 1600s, a French chef experimented with small cakes he stacked together and held in place with a white sugar icing. And before the U.S. Civil War, the wedding cake was actually a fruitcake.

Ask the baker if there's a deposit on the cake stands and pillars. Also, check how the wedding cake pieces (plastic pillars, the layer pieces holding the cake together) are to be returned. Will the caterer take care of that for you, or you are responsible?

Finally, ask if the caterer cuts and serves the cake for you. Again, there may be a charge for that, but cutting a wedding cake is an art.

For more help planning your cake, turn to the "Wedding Cake Worksheet" in Appendix A.

These individual cakes will be served to guests, with ribbons attached, holding charms to pull for good luck.

(PHOTO BY MELANIE MAUER)

Here's a cake done in gold
and silver icing. Looks
like a big gift to open!

(PHOTO BY GARBO PRODUCTIONS)

The Groom's Cake

The groom's cake has become an important part of
the wedding reception. These days groom's cakes
come in all kinds of shapes, sizes, flavors, and themes
such as basketball and football themes. One groom
who loved to play bridge had his groom's cake
designed like a huge hand of cards. And remember
the red velvet armadillo in the movie *Steel Magnolias?*
That was an original (if not odd) groom's cake. As
these few examples show, you're limited only by your
imagination!

Chocolate seems to be a very popular flavor with
grooms, but I've also seen cheesecakes served with
luscious fruit toppings as a groom's cake.

This groom's cake made to look like a school bus
goes with his career—he's a teacher.

(PHOTO BY COLTER PHOTOGRAPHY)

Those Luscious Libations

Traditional etiquette says only that you must offer your guests something to eat and something to drink at the reception. If that something to drink is alcohol, that's your choice and yours alone. Nonalcoholic beverages are certainly appropriate and should be included.

If you're considering offering liquor at your reception, become familiar with the terminology now so you can ask your vendor intelligent questions. For help on planning your options, see the "Liquor Worksheet" in Appendix A.

Let's take a look at your options:

Limited bar. You limit what is served to the guests. Often a limited bar features both wine and beer, plus soft drinks or maybe punch.

A limited time bar. You limit the time the bar remains open. For example, if your reception is scheduled to start with cocktails at 6:30 and dinner is served at 7:30, you may decide to have the bar open from 6:30 to 7:30, close it from 7:30 until 9, and then open it again at 9 until a half hour before the reception ends. You pay the bill with a limited bar.

Open bar. You can offer a full bar outfitted with the liquor you choose. The bar consists of mixed drinks, wine, beer, and soft drinks. You also can choose to serve some after-dinner liquors. With an open bar, you pay the bill.

Cash bar. If you offer a cash bar at your reception, guests pay for their own drinks. You may offer wine and soft drinks and then if guests want something else in the way of

Mint juleps are a southern tradition. Use your heritage when planning your reception.

(PHOTO BY MELANIE MAUER)

liquor, they can buy it from the bartender. Many people feel that a cash bar is insulting to their guests. You wouldn't make your guests pay for a drink in your home, so why make them pay for one at your reception? However, if guests are paying for their own drinks, they may not be as free with the liquor and will watch their consumption. It's your call.

Teddy's Tips

Don't take your responsibilities lightly when serving liquor. Be sure you have a reputable liquor dealer serving the alcohol. Liability laws differ from state to state, and you or the host needs to be informed on what your state's liabilities are.

Signature drinks are a big trend these days. These martini glasses are waiting to be filled with the bride's favorite martini.

(PHOTO BY MELANIE MAUER)

THE LEAST YOU NEED TO KNOW

- It's possible to work with the caterer without blowing your budget. Be sure to go into the initial consultation with a good idea of the kind of reception you want.

- Always give an accurate count to the caterer; never guess at numbers for your guaranteed count.

- There are nearly as many choices in wedding and groom's cakes as there are brides and grooms!

- If you decide to serve liquor at your reception, become familiar with your options so you can make an educated choice.

CHAPTER 8

All Dressed Up and Somewhere to Go

In This Chapter

- Shopping for the wedding gown and accessories
- Passing down family gowns: to wear or not to wear?
- Dressing the bridesmaids
- Decking out the men in your wedding party
- Getting to the church on time: creative transportation ideas

Finding the right bridal gown and then trying to outfit the bridesmaids can sometimes seem like an insurmountable task. It doesn't have to be, though, if you take it one step at a time. This chapter guides you down the aisles of bridal shops to help you find your dream gown, accessories, and bridesmaids' dresses.

Also in this chapter, I help the men in your wedding party choose their attire, and I give you some creative ideas for wedding transportation.

This bride is wearing a mermaid-style gown. It looks like they're practicing their first dance.

(PHOTO BY GARBO PRODUCTIONS)

This pretty bride is wearing an ornate embroidered gown, complemented simply with a pair of earrings.

(PHOTO BY WYANT PHOTOGRAPHY)

Cinderella for a Day

Your wedding day is an opportunity for you to become a princess, to be the center of attention, to be *oohed* and *ahhed* at, and of course, to wear the most magnificent dress you'll ever own: the dress of your dreams. Although the bride dons this dress for only one day of her life, it's important that it's just perfect. You don't want to look at your wedding photos a few years from now and proclaim, "Why in the world did I wear that?"

Wedding Woes

It's not a wise move to order your gown from a shop advertising that it's going out of business, thinking you'll get a bargain. If you can buy the gown off the rack, that's fine. But don't put down a deposit and allow the store to order your gown.

This bride has on a full-length veil and long gloves and is carrying a calla lily bouquet. Bridal gloves are making a comeback.

(PHOTO BY WYANT PHOTOGRAPHY)

Before you begin your shopping, ask yourself the following:

- What gown might flatter you the most?
- What style of gown will help set the mood or theme of the wedding?
- How formal will the wedding be?

- What time of year are you getting married?
- Do you feel comfortable with the bridal salon and its staff?
- How important is comfort to you? This one you really need to think about when you have a few gowns to choose from.

This bride has a full cathedral-length veil with a chapel-length train. The veil extends beyond the train.

(PHOTO BY WYANT PHOTOGRAPHY)

A closer view of the gown's cap sleeve.

(PHOTO BY WYANT PHOTOGRAPHY)

This couple takes a walk. Notice how the bride's gown crosses at the waistline. The groom wears a traditional tux.

(PHOTO BY WYANT PHOTOGRAPHY)

Thinking Ahead

You should order your gown at least 6 months before the wedding. It doesn't take 6 months for your gown to arrive at the shop, but with possible delays in shipping, manufacturing problems, and alterations, it's best to be on the safe side. If you don't have 6 months' lead time, be sure you mention that to the shop. Several bridal gown companies specialize in short order times.

By Appointment Only

Be sure you check with the bridal shops to see if you need to make an appointment before your visit. If the shop doesn't accept appointments, ask for the best time to shop. Saturdays, for example, are often very busy days for bridal shops; try to shop on another day of the week.

Oh, It's *So* You!

When shopping for your wedding gown, look at many different styles of dresses. You might be really surprised to find that a gown style you thought would not complement you really does.

You'll have several options in terms of style, cut, fabric, and adornments. On your first shopping trip, try on a few different styles to get a feel for what works for you.

Here's some additional advice to keep in mind when shopping for a gown:

- Shop with an open mind. Just because you have your heart set on a sheath gown with a detachable train, don't be afraid to try on the gown with the flowing skirt and cowl neckline.

- A second (or third) opinion is always a good idea. Many mothers dream of the day they can take their daughters wedding-dress shopping. Take one or two people with you when you shop, maybe your maid of honor or another close bridesmaid. These ladies usually enjoy gown shopping with their bride friend.

- Don't think all stores are the same—shop around. You might even find the same or similar dress elsewhere but realize you like the service or location of a particular shop better.

- Look through bridal magazines to see the latest styles and trends.

- Get referrals from recent brides.

For help in shopping wisely, turn to the "Wedding Gown and Bridesmaids' Dresses Worksheet" in Appendix A.

❀ Bouquet Toss

The traditional color of a bridal gown is white, representing purity, but that wasn't always the case. In ancient times, red and other bright colors were favored. In the mid-nineteenth century, Empress Eugenie, wife of Napoleon III, broke the medieval tradition of wearing a brightly colored wedding gown and chose white. In the Victorian period, brides from affluent U.S. families began wearing white gowns to show that they could afford to have a special dress they would wear only one time. Most women simply wore the best dress they had at the time. A white gown did not come to represent purity until the twentieth century.

⚭ Teddy's Tips

If you don't dress up when you go bridal-dress shopping, at least take a pair of dress shoes with you. Have your hair fixed appropriately, and add a little makeup. It's really hard to judge how you might look on your wedding day if you're wearing tennis shoes with your hair in a ponytail. Time spent checking your hair and makeup and having the right shoes along makes a big difference in what you see in the mirror.

A lovely bride against the ocean view.

(PHOTO BY NORTHERN LIGHTS PHOTOGRAPHY)

Don't Veil the Truth

You might be surprised at all the options you have when it comes to a veil—different weights of fabric, choices of trimmings, and, of course, length.

Here are the common choices in veil lengths:

- **Fingertip veil.** Just brushes the shoulders and frames the face.

- **Elbow-length veil.** Brushes the elbows.

- **Chapel-length veil.** Measures 3 yards long (9 feet).

- **Cathedral-length veil.** Measures 4 yards long (12 feet).

If your gown doesn't have a long train (or a train at all), you might want to consider having a longer veil to act as a train. Try on different styles to be sure you get the best match for both your gown and your hairstyle.

You don't have to wear a veil at all. It depends on the formality of the wedding and your personal preference. Some brides opt for flowers in their hair or decorative hair ornaments. Others wear a veil for the ceremony and then remove it for the reception, leaving on the headpiece.

Bouquet Toss

Before the sixteenth century, unmarried women wore veils as a sign of modesty, and married women wore them to show that they were submissive to their husbands. My, how things change!

This gown has embroidery work all along the train. The groom wears a tux with the newer-look long tie.

(PHOTO BY WYANT PHOTOGRAPHY)

The Glass Slippers

You might think shoes aren't something you need to devote much time to—who's going to see them anyway? But think about how many hours you're going to be on your feet! I can't emphasize this enough: be sure your shoes are comfortable!

Brides often choose a lovely pair of formal shoes for the ceremony and then slip on a pair of ballet slippers for the reception. Their feet are exceptionally appreciative.

Also popular are tennis shoes trimmed with ribbons and lace to dress them up. These can be purchased at many bridal shops or through catalogs and can help the bride dance all night.

Wedding Woes

Wait until you've decided on a gown before you begin picking out your veil or other headpiece. You wouldn't want an unflattering veil to overpower the beauty of the dress.

The Final Touches

Here are some added final touches to consider:

- Jewelry—just the right piece to accent the gown

- Long gloves if your gown is strapless

- A small matching clutch bag for the reception

- A shawl for cool evenings

- A warm wrap, either velvet or fake-fur, for cold climates

This bride chose to wear flowers in her hair instead of a veil.

(PHOTO BY MELANIE MAUER)

This bride poses for a formal portrait in the church. She's wearing gloves with her strapless gown and a full-length veil.

(PHOTO BY COLTER PHOTOGRAPHY)

Wedding Woes

Alterations can be very expensive; always know up front what the shop charges for the service. Your best bet is to try to remain approximately the size you were when you ordered your gown. If you're expecting a large weight loss, either have your gown made locally or wait until you're closer to your desired weight before you order. Never order a gown in a smaller size, expecting that you'll lose the extra pounds. It's much easier to take in the gown than let out the seams!

This lace-covered gown is completed with a simple pair of pearl earrings.

(PHOTO BY WYANT PHOTOGRAPHY)

Service with a Smile

If you know others who have used a certain bridal shop, ask those brides how they were treated:

- Were all their questions answered satisfactorily?

- How did the gown look when it was ready to be picked up or when it arrived at the ceremony site? Were the sleeves stuffed with tissue?

- Was a *bodice form* used? Was the train tied up or draped over the hanger?

- Did the shop explain how to bustle the gown?

- Were alterations included or an extra cost? (This is a very important and potentially costly question.)

Be sure the shop takes your measurements before ordering your gown. Formalwear runs small, so don't be surprised if you require a larger size than you wear in ready-wear clothing.

Nuptial Notes

A **bodice form** is a piece of cardboard shaped like a woman's upper body that the shop places in the bodice of your gown to keep it free of wrinkles and looking fresh. This protects the gown during travel time from the shop to your home or ceremony site.

If It Was Good Enough for Mom …

Sally Lorensen Conant, Ph.D., president of Orange Restoration Labs in Orange, Connecticut, offers the following advice and ideas if you're considering wearing a family gown—either your mother's, your grandmother's, your sister's, or even a friend's gown:

> For the bride who values tradition and sentiment, a family gown may be just right. Family gowns come in all sizes and shapes, and they can be fitted to all sizes and shapes. In fact, we know a bridal shop that can make a gown as many as 12 sizes larger! Always make the decision to wear a family gown, whether it belongs to your mother or your favorite aunt or even a close family friend, based on the meaning the gown has for you and whether the style suits you—not on the way it fits or its condition. A specialist can restore even a yellowed, badly stained gown to the true color, and a talented dressmaker can reshape almost any gown to your size.

Several companies offer gown restoration services, which can make your mother's or grandmother's yellowed gown beautiful again. Call the Wedding Gown Specialists Association at 1-800-501-5005 for a cleaner/preservation specialist in your area.

Pretty Maids All in a Row

Shopping for your bridesmaids' dresses should be a pleasant experience. Let me offer these words of wisdom to help guide you:

Shop only with your maid of honor and your mother or another close friend.

Take into account the physical sizes of your maids so the style you pick works for all the girls.

Try to choose something the girls can wear another time. These days manufacturers are making this task easier by offering dresses that have separate tops and skirts and a variety of different styles that can be worn for other occasions.

Use your best judgment, and try to choose something with a reasonable price tag.

A trend now is for the bride to choose the fabric and each bridesmaid select a pattern complementary to her. Then all the dresses are made, each different but all the same color.

Wedding Woes

Beware the unserviceable gown! Before you actually purchase a dress, look at the care label. Federal law requires manufacturers to put labels into clothing describing the proper care for the garment. Some labels actually say "Do Not Wash" and "Do Not Dry Clean." Unless you have absolutely no interest in what happens to your gown after the wedding, better pass up a dress with these labels.

Dressed to Kill: Formal Wear for Men

The groom and his men want to look just as handsome as the bride and her attendants want to look beautiful. Take some time to look through bridal magazines to get a feel for what's available for the men in your wedding party. (Be sure to use the "Tuxedo Worksheet" in Appendix A.) There are hundreds of tuxedo styles, ties, shirts, vests, and colors from which you can choose.

Select the style and brand of tuxedo that will complement the wedding theme, the time of day, and what the bridesmaids are wearing.

This groom is dressed in a navy tux with silver accents.
(PHOTO BY COLTER PHOTOGRAPHY)

Accent with Color

Prints, gold and silver threads on black vests, along with accents in ties and cummerbunds are appearing more frequently these days. We are also seeing the popular no-tie neckline for men. That style neckline comes with a type of broach to be worn at the neckline and thus no tie. White tie is still considered very formal and is a most appropriate look for a formal wedding after 6 o'clock in the evening.

Bouquet Toss

One ancient tradition was to dress the bridesmaids and groomsmen like the bride and groom so the evil demons would be confused if they tried to put a curse on the couple.

Right Down to Their Feet

Be sure the men have dress shoes. You don't want them dressed to the hilt in a wonderful tuxedo, yet wearing cowboy boots or tennis shoes. They need to have a pair of black or gray (depending on the color of tuxedo) leather or patent leather dress shoes. Also, white socks just don't complement the ensemble for someone wearing a dark suit or tuxedo! Be sure the groomsmen have black dress socks to go with their formal shoes.

Getting the Suit on Time

The men should order their formal wear about 2 to 3 months before the wedding. Look in the Yellow Pages under "Wedding Services and Supplies" or "Formal Wear" for listings of retailers that offer tuxedos (formal wear) for rent. You can also purchase tuxedos, but they are expensive. Unless you plan to use one extensively, it's cheaper to rent a tuxedo when you need it.

Buying in Bulk

Your rented tuxedo is a package deal. In other words, you receive the jacket, trousers, choice of shirt, tie, vest or cummerbund, studs, and cuff links for one price.

Shoes may be rented also, but that's usually an extra charge. Sometimes colored handkerchiefs are included to add color to the outfit (they go in the breast pocket, not the back pocket).

Many stores offer some kind of special or discount on tuxedo rentals: "Rent six tuxedos, get the groom's free," or maybe, "Rent your tuxedos from us, and receive your limousine rental free." Always ask about specials.

Teddy's Tips

It's a good idea to carry collar extenders in your emergency kit in case one of the guys' shirts is too tight around his neck. This little contraption can add an inch or so to make his life—and breathing—a little easier.

This groom added a tiny silver holder for his boutonniere. It looks really sharp.

(PHOTO BY FOTOBRICENO)

Arriving in Style

The mode of transportation you plan to use for your wedding day is one detail that's easy to overlook. With a little planning, however, this item can add a unique flair to your special day. The "Special Transportation Worksheet" in Appendix A can help you in this area.

Many couples use special transportation to take them from the ceremony to the reception. Other couples use special forms of transportation from home to the ceremony, and some couples use special transportation to take them from the reception to their wedding-night destination. It's a personal choice; be creative, but stay within your budget.

Here are some fun transportation ideas:

- A limousine (Elegant and classy, riding in a limousine can make you feel like a celebrity.)

- A Rolls Royce

- A classic car (a convertible, for example)

- A horse and carriage

- A motorcycle (Yes, I said a motorcycle!)

- A trolley car (for the entire wedding party, too)

- A bus (for the whole wedding party)

You can find most of these forms of transportation in the Yellow Pages under "Car Rentals" or "Car Clubs." Maybe you have a friend who owns a classic car who would let you use it for your "getaway."

Talk about lift-off! What a way to arrive or exit your reception.

(PHOTO BY DARWIN'S PHOTOGRAPHY)

A white carriage awaits this couple as they take some private time together.

(PHOTO BY WYANT PHOTOGRAPHY)

Be Creative!

Perhaps my trophy for the most unique mode of wedding transportation I have ever witnessed goes to a couple I worked with several years ago. They had a beautiful garden wedding followed by a lovely garden reception. The home was in the country, and we were surrounded by trees, flowers, and the beauty of nature. When I asked them if they were going to leave from the reception in any special form, they assured me that they had nothing in mind and would just leave in their car. When the time came, the bride's brother appeared with a small tractor (yes, I said tractor) that had a box on the back for hauling. The couple took one look at the tractor, hopped onboard, and off they rode into the sunset (or the field, or wherever their car was parked).

Use your imagination. Make your grand exit in style, but make it in *your* style. As always, remember to ask many questions of the various vendors and to get referrals.

If you live near the ocean, a boat makes sense.

(PHOTO BY MONIQUE FEIL)

THE LEAST YOU NEED TO KNOW

- Try to allow at least 6 months for ordering and receiving your wedding gown. If you don't have that much time, it might cost you a bit more.

- If you're considering wearing a family gown, check with a gown restoration service, which can make an old gown look beautiful again.

- When choosing bridesmaids' dresses, think about the attendants' physical attributes and coloring, as well as what they can reasonably afford.

- The groom's formal wear should complement the style of wedding you're planning as well as the bridal gown.

- Be creative when deciding on the transportation you'll use for your wedding day. Use your imagination and have fun with this decision.

CHAPTER 9

Snapdragons and Song

IN THIS CHAPTER

- Getting the flowers you want—within your budget

- Creating the "look" you want for your wedding

- Finding inspiration with centerpiece ideas

- Making the musical choices for your wedding

- Hiring the right musician for your tastes

In this chapter, I focus on two important aspects of your wedding: the flowers and the music. Both items are filled with choices. I cover what you need to include in your floral order, from bouquets to centerpieces; give you hints on how to get the best value for your wedding floral dollars; and give you some extra tips on how to spice up the reception site.

I also look at your options for the music for your wonderful celebration. Music can really set the mood, and you want to be sure it's not only the mood you want, but also a mood well spent!

These flowers are stealing the show!

(PHOTO BY NORTHERN LIGHTS PHOTOGRAPHY)

These tall iron vases hold up large, stately bouquets of flowers. Notice the green glassware, which matches the linens.

(PHOTO BY GARBO PRODUCTIONS)

Beautiful flowers everywhere. And they smelled good, too!

(PHOTO BY EMILY'S IMAGES)

❀ Bouquet Toss

The very first types of bridal bouquets included not only flowers, but also herbs and spices. Especially popular were strong-scented ones, such as garlic, which were thought to ward off evil spirits. Various kinds of flowers have different meanings. Ivy represents fidelity, lily of the valley represents purity, red roses mean love, violets represent modesty, forget-me-nots mean true love, orange blossoms represent fertility and happiness, and myrtle is the symbol of virginity.

Working With a Florist

Under normal circumstances, you don't really have to decide on flowers until 2 or 3 months before the wedding. However, if you're being married in a prime wedding season (May, June, or August), or if you're being married around a holiday (Christmas, Valentine's Day, or Mother's Day weekend), it's wise to reserve your florist early. Some florists service only one or two weddings a weekend during the peak seasons because they're such labor-intensive productions.

The centerpiece for this fall reception is enhanced by the fall-color chocolates on the table.

(PHOTO BY COLTER PHOTOGRAPHY)

This reception venue lends itself to the height of the centerpieces. These centerpieces were designed to fit the height of this venue. Gorgeous!

(PHOTO BY WYANT PHOTOGRAPHY)

Here are some suggestions for working with the florist:

Ask if he is familiar with the ceremony and reception site before you meet. If he isn't, ask if he could visit the site so he knows how it looks so he can better assist you.

Take pictures with you from magazines or other weddings so the florist has an idea of your likes.

Ask if she uses a contract (some small-town florists don't) and if she'll do an estimate for you.

Ask if there's a delivery and set-up fee or if that's built into the floral charge.

Ask if he'll transport the ceremony flowers from the church to the reception site. Get your money's worth out of your floral bill!

If you're using silk flowers, ask to see and smell the silk flowers. Some silk flowers have a distinct odor to them.

Be sure the florist knows if you or your groom has any floral allergies.

Teddy's Tips

Petals, either fresh or dried, are a wonderful alternative to birdseed when showering the couple as they leave the ceremony. The flower petals don't get caught in your clothes and hair, and they smell wonderful. They are natural as well, so you don't have to worry about the environment. Check with your florist.

Pretty bouquets all in a row.

(PHOTO BY WYANT PHOTOGRAPHY)

A good florist will do the following:

- Assist you in determining what flowers will work for your wedding, given the time of year and your wedding style

- Offer suggestions and ideas

- Stay within your floral budget

- Ask for a picture of your gown, the bridesmaids' gowns, and color swatches

- Explain their pricing system, including if they require a deposit

- Provide references if requested

- Label corsages so you know who gets what

Buds of Beauty

Flowers used during the ceremony are divided into two sections. One set is referred to as "body flowers" and includes the bouquets, boutonnieres, and corsages. The second set is the flowers used at the sites, both ceremony and reception.

These bridesmaids' bouquets wait in vases while the cake is assembled in the background.

(PHOTO BY NORTHERN LIGHTS PHOTOGRAPHY)

Bouquets and "Boots"

The two main body flowers for weddings are the bouquets and the *boutonnieres*, or "boots," as they're more fondly referred to. When choosing these flowers, first consider the style and color of the bridesmaids' bouquets and the overall theme of your wedding. Show your florist samples of your colors and fabrics, a picture of the dresses, and describe to him what you envision.

Some sample styles of bouquets for your maids are nosegays; small crescent shape; arm bouquet (simply put, it lies in the crook of your arm); or a single, long-stemmed flower, maybe tied with an elegant ribbon. Let the florist help you with your decisions.

The florist needs to keep several points in mind as he designs your bridal arrangement. First, he should note your physical size, as your bouquet needs to correspond with your size. Next, the florist will want to see a picture of your gown. The bouquet is meant to accent the gown, not take away from it. He can also tell from the lines of the gown how the lines in the bouquet should run. Remember, this is an art form, and it takes a good, experienced florist to pull the total look of a wedding together.

Nuptial Notes

A **boutonniere** is a small flower the men in the wedding wear on their tux lapel. Tradition says the groom's boutonniere should be taken from the bride's bouquet. Today we don't pull flowers from the bride's bouquet and pin them on the groom, but his flower should match the bride's.

This ribbon-wrapped bouquet is also wrapped with beads and pearls. Absolutely beautiful!

(PHOTO BY RENAISSANCE PHOTOGRAPHY BY R.D. HUNT)

A pink rose bouquet with a silver monogram holder is very classy.

(PHOTO BY MELANIE MAUER)

Angels among us. This flower girl stands quietly wearing her rose halo, a popular way to use flowers to dress up the little girls in your wedding party.

(PHOTO BY BROADWAY PHOTOGRAPHY)

This mother is ready to go down the aisle with her small bouquet in a tussy mussy.

(PHOTO BY BROADWAY PHOTOGRAPHY

You need boutonnieres for all the men in your wedding party, including the fathers, grandfathers, ushers, groomsmen, ring bearer (make his small!), and, of course, the groom. The groom's should be different from the others. Tradition suggests that his boutonniere be made of some of the flowers from the bride's bouquet.

The final body flowers you need to consider are corsages or something for the mothers and grandmothers to wear. Today, many mothers opt for something other than a corsage. They prefer to carry a long-stemmed flower down the aisle than to have something pinned to the dress they just paid a small fortune for and don't want pinholes in it. Grandmothers usually prefer corsages.

Petals and More

The flowers you choose to use at your ceremony site will depend on many factors. First, you have to consider the all-important budget. Second, think about whether the site really needs a lot of décor. Many churches are lovely just by themselves. Adding small amounts of flowers such as some pew pieces or some candles might be all you need. In Jewish ceremonies, it's popular to put flowers in the chuppah. It all depends on your site, your personal preference, and your budget.

Whatever you decide to do with flowers at the ceremony site, be sure they can be moved to the reception site. You're spending some bucks on those flowers, so you might as well get the most use out of those dollars.

Bouquet Toss

Bold color in bouquets is very big these days. Even bride's bouquet, which were once thought to be only white, are now featuring bold colors. Look at some of the floral pictures in this book, and you will see how bold the color for flowers can get.

This dramatic aisle is draped with silver fabric and vases of candles and calla lilies.

(PHOTO BY WYANT PHOTOGRAPHY)

These beautiful silver candle stands holding the ceremony flowers are very elegant.

(PHOTO BY BRAD BASKER)

From Simple to Sensational: Centerpiece Ideas

For any type of reception besides a cake-and-punch reception, you need to provide tables where your guests can sit. The layout of your facility, the time of day and style of the reception, the table size, and the number of guests you want to seat are all considerations you must keep in mind as you decide on centerpieces.

Here are some ideas for centerpieces:

- For a simple, inexpensive idea, use some votive candles and greenery and sprinkle some glitter on the table. If you're on a tight budget, ask some good friends to set this up for you.

- Rent some table candelabras and have the florist arrange some flowers at the base.

- Rent tall pedestal centerpieces (the stem is about 36 inches) and have the florist put flowers in the top container. This works well in a large room with very high ceilings. Also, this can be mixed with lower, less elaborate centerpieces on every other or every third table.

- Group several different-size vases with a simple arrangement in each and add some votive candles.

- Wrap empty boxes in Christmas paper and stack them in the middle of the table. Perfect for a Christmas wedding!

This centerpiece is made of floating flowers and candles. Notice that the table is named for the Shedd Aquarium. Naming tables for various subjects is a way to make your wedding more personal.

(PHOTO BY GARBO PRODUCTIONS)

This centerpiece is so gorgeous. It contains several different flowers, using all different shades of pinks.

(PHOTO BY EMILY'S IMAGES)

- Use individual wedding cakes as your centerpiece at each table. Have the baker make a simple 9-inch-round cake, ice it like the wedding cake, and place it on a pedestal to use as the centerpiece. When you cut your first piece from your wedding cake, your guests can follow suit at their tables.

- Lay wide colored ribbon down the center of the table. Top it with candles and greenery and maybe some rose petals.

- Add things like a decorative napkin fold (such as a fan fold) or other unusual napkin placement to make the tables unique.

- A favor can add to the overall table décor. (See Chapter 12 for more on favors.)

- Use a variety of candles—some tapers, some pillars of different heights, some votives, etc.—to create a warm glow at the table.

- Bowls with goldfish are popular. Surround the bowls with votive candles for a warm glow.

- Cluster hurricane globes with either tapers or pillar candles in the center of the table.

- Hurricane globes laid on their sides with flowers spilling from both open ends make an interesting centerpiece.

This simple bouquet of multi-colored pink roses looks nice against the black runner.

(PHOTO BY COLTER PHOTOGRAPHY)

- Tightly pack tapers and flowers inside the base of a hurricane globe.

- Polished rocks mixed with a variety of candles add a natural element to your table.

- A rose bowl with a single open rose in the bottom of the bowl is simple but elegant.

Be sure to check the "Floral Worksheet" in Appendix A for help organizing your floral needs.

Making Beautiful Music

Music completes your wedding atmosphere. Because it stays in the background, music is also one aspect of wedding planning that's easy to overlook, especially for the ceremony. But you must reserve wedding music early, both for the ceremony and the reception.

Waltzing Down the Aisle

What do you and your groom like in music? Do you have an organ in mind, or would you prefer something like a harp or a guitar? There are all kinds of ways to make music a fun and meaningful part of your wedding ceremony.

Typical instruments and vocals for wedding ceremonies include the following:

- Organ
- Piano
- Violin
- String quartet
- Flute
- Harp
- Trumpet
- Small chamber orchestra
- Choir
- Soloist
- Duet

Visit the musician in charge of your ceremony music. If you're having the ceremony in a religious setting, that person will most likely be the minister of music, the director of music, or the organist or pianist. Talk with this person about your likes and dislikes and what you would like to hear on your wedding day. Ask for

ideas as well. Many times, if you meet in the facility, the musician can play a few bars of a certain piece so you can hear the music. If you don't have access to a musician who can accommodate you, visit your local music store and purchase some wedding music CDs.

Wedding Woes

Try to use live musicians for your wedding ceremony. Using taped music may save you money, but it can also be risky. If you go this route, be sure you have someone reliable to run your CD player. I still remember the 14-year-old young man who was supposed to hit the Play button on the CD player and got so excited that he not only hit the Play button, but he also knocked over the candelabra, which burned a hole in the church's carpet!

Teddy's Tips

Try to arrange to see the musician or group perform live at another venue before deciding to book them for your wedding. You'll also be able to judge their poise and rapport with the audience.

A string quartet plays for the cocktail hour—a nice touch.
(PHOTO BY WYANT PHOTOGRAPHY)

Some popular choices for processional music include the following:

- "Bridal Chorus" by Lohengrin ("Here Comes the Bride")
- "The Wedding March" from Mendelssohn's *A Midsummer Night's Dream*
- "Rondo," the *Masterpiece Theatre* theme, by Mouret
- "Prince of Denmark's March" by Clarke
- "Fanfare" from *The Triumphant* by Couperin
- "Sarabande" from *Suite No. 11* by Handel
- "Trumpet Tune" by Purcell
- "Trumpet Voluntary" by Clarke
- "Water Music" by Handel
- "The Wedding March" from *The Sound of Music* by Rogers and Hammerstein

And for the ceremony music:

- "Jesu, Joy of Man's Desiring" by Bach
- "Canon in D Minor" by Pachebel
- "A Wedding Prayer" by Williams
- "Wedding Song" by Stookey
- "One Hand, One Heart" from *West Side Story* by Bernstein and Sondheim
- "The Lord's Prayer" by Malotte

- "Sunrise, Sunset" from *Fiddler on the Roof* by Harnick and Bock
- "On the Wings of Love" by Jeffrey Osborne
- "The Hands of Time (Brian's Song)" by Michel LeGrand
- "Somewhere" from *West Side Story* by Bernstein and Sondheim

Party Music

Although certainly not mandatory, music is a nice addition to the reception. This can be as simple or as elaborate as your budget and tastes dictate. A pianist playing soft background music is nice for the simple cake-and-punch reception, or you might choose to have a 20-piece orchestra in the ballroom playing the sounds of Glenn Miller for a formal dinner and dance reception. It goes back to your personal tastes and what style of wedding you want. Ask family and friends who have used a particular musician or group before for their recommendations.

Here are a few things to keep in mind when you discuss your reception music with the vendor:

What are their rates? Do they require a deposit?

Ask for a tape of the musician or group if you're unfamiliar with the music.

Check the contracts. How many breaks do the musicians require, and how often do they take those breaks? Do they have access to taped music to play during those breaks? It's nice for the guests to hear some soft music playing in the background rather than dead silence.

Will they announce you or help with the garter and bouquet toss?

How long will they play? Will they stay past their end time if you request them to do so, and how much will the extra time cost?

If a style of music isn't working, will they try something different? Your dance floor should be active most of the evening, which is usually a sign of a good reception. For that to happen, a band must be able to "read" the crowd.

Wedding Woes

The music for your wedding ceremony needs the approval of the church or the officiant performing the service. Always check with the ceremony site before you finalize any plans. Most places welcome all types of musical instruments, but some are very strict.

Ask if they carry liability insurance. Most facilities require this of all vendors, but especially the musicians.

Ask if the band offers a song list from which you can make selections. Will they play a special song if asked?

The musicians should be in tune (bad pun!) with the volume level during the reception. Tactfully ask about how they regulate the volume control. If you ask them to turn down the volume, will they cooperate? Some guests prefer to sit at their tables and chat with family and friends. If they can't carry on a conversation over the music, it's too loud. You want the volume loud enough for those on the dance floor to appreciate, but not so loud as to make other guests shout to each other at their tables.

A DJ (short for disc jockey) is another avenue for your reception music. Any form of music makers at your reception can make or break the party. Be sure you've seen a DJ's performance and understand what he will and won't do. Read the contract carefully. Note how long he will play and how many breaks he will take. Check out whether he will need any extra electricity at the reception. Be sure he will be dressed appropriately as well.

Music can add a wonderful aspect to both your ceremony and your reception. Make wise musical choices for both situations, as your choices can frame your wedding day and set the mood for all to enjoy! Remember to check the "Musicians Worksheet" in Appendix A for help.

THE LEAST YOU NEED TO KNOW

- Allow the florist some freedom in designing what will work best for your budget and your overall expectations.

- Flowers used during the ceremony include bouquets, boutonnieres, and corsages. Flowers used at the ceremony and reception sites include centerpieces and other decorative arrangements.

- Centerpieces can be as simple or as elaborate as your taste and budget dictates.

- When choosing music for your ceremony and reception, consider all options.

- Music is a special part of any wedding, so consider what you and your partner like—and book early!

CHAPTER 10

Pretty as a Picture: Photographers and Videographers

IN THIS CHAPTER

- Choosing the right photographer
- Looking at styles of wedding photography
- Understanding the contract
- Finding the right videographer
- Deciding on the best time to take pictures

In this chapter, we take a look at what's out there and what choices you have in the photography and video industry. These two elements of your wedding day are so important. Don't take shortcuts here if they are a high priority for you. Shop wisely for these vendors.

Also in this chapter, I talk about when to take those precious pictures and what options you have.

Photographers can create all sorts of moods and emotions with the camera.

(PHOTO BY COLTER PHOTOGRAPHY)

Memories to Last a Lifetime

Photography is an expensive undertaking for most couples. You want good pictures that capture your special day, but that means you're going to have to spend some time investigating your choices now and to allow enough money in your budget to accomplish that goal.

So Many Questions, So Little Time

When you meet with the photographer, you need to consider several items. First, look at the quality of the photographer's work. Ask yourself:

- Does the photographer's work capture the moment?

- Look through the photographer's display albums. Do the pictures express the romance of the day?

A priceless series of photos this photographer captured on film.

(PHOTOS BY BROADWAY PHOTOGRAPHY)

The bride is looking for her groom.

She sees him!

What a smile!

Ah ... at last they meet for the first time on their wedding day.

- What photos catch your eye? Are they straight shots? Do the pictures tell a story?

- Find out whether the photographer will take candid shots; many photographers won't.

- Is the photographer available on your wedding date? What is the fee?

- What kinds of packages does he offer?

- Are the photos you're viewing the work of the photographer you're actually hiring? (Sometimes the photos shown could be his assistant's or associate's.)

Wedding Woes

Be sure to find out what kind of contract the photographer uses and read it carefully. Does the contract include a time limit? You want to avoid having to pay overtime to your photographer; overtime can add up to big money very quickly.

Teddy's Tips

Always take care of your support staff—photographer, videographer, DJ or band, and coordinators—by offering them food and a special place at the reception for them to regroup.

Do You Get That Warm, Fuzzy Feeling?

One of the most important questions you have to ask is whether you both feel comfortable with this photographer. Be honest with yourselves. You will spend a lot of time on your wedding day with this person; if you don't like him or her, for whatever reason, it will show in your pictures.

What's in a Picture?

You might have several different styles of wedding photography to choose from. The type of photography a particular photographer offers depends on his ability, experience, and personal choice, but you'll be better off if you at least know the differences and can understand the terminology.

Portraiture

Portraiture is probably one of the most common types of photography, although you might not know it by this name. This refers to the formal posed pictures at the ceremony site and reception. There isn't much spontaneity here, but the pictures can be almost perfect, depending on the photographer.

Natural Light

This type of photography does not use artificial light. In other words, no flash is used. The photographer uses what light is available naturally to create the image. When done well, a natural light photograph reminds you of a fine work of art.

This couple is posed against the natural setting of lush woods and a creek.

(PHOTO BY WYANT PHOTOGRAPHY)

This is a soft focus in the background, with the color of the flowers more defined.

(PHOTO BY NORTHERN LIGHTS PHOTOGRAPHY)

Photojournalistic

Wedding photography done in the photojournalistic style takes its technique from the news media. The photographer, through pictures, tells the story of your wedding on film. Instead of posing pictures to create a mood, the photographer follows the people and mood of the event and captures it on film as it unfolds. It is a huge trend with couples all over the country, as well as the mixing of color photos with black-and-white images and sepia tones and black and white images with color added.

Black-and-white photography with color accents added is very popular.

(PHOTO BY WYANT PHOTOGRAPHY)

This is one of my favorites. It appears that these Gerber daisies are hanging in midair. (They're actually on wire, marking the aisle.)

(PHOTO BY MONIQUE FEIL)

Read the Fine Print: Understanding Contracts

It's very important to understand the kind of contract the photographer uses and exactly what the price includes. Be sure you understand this, and don't be afraid to ask questions!

Here are some questions to ask the photographer:

- Does the contract include an album?

- How does the photographer get the proofs to you?

- Does he use a CD format for you to view your proofs?

- When you buy a package, is there a time limit on how long the photographer is available? (It's important to consider whether the contract includes a time limit.)

- Does he require food at the reception?

- Does he bring assistants?

- What is his dress for the wedding?

- How long after the wedding will you have your finished album?

A quiet moment for this couple.

(PHOTO BY WYANT PHOTOGRAPHY)

Love a sunset—and this one is beautiful!

(PHOTO BY NORTHERN LIGHTS PHOTOGRAPHY)

For more help determining your photography needs, turn to the "Photography Worksheet" in Appendix A.

Good wedding photography is meant to last a lifetime. You want to choose a photographer who can help you capture on film all the wonderful emotions of your big day. You want someone who treats you with respect and sensitivity, and you want all this without even noticing that the photographer is in the room.

When to Take the Wedding Pictures

One of the biggest dilemmas couples face today is how to work in time for the wedding pictures. The question you and your groom have to ask yourselves is, "Do we want to see each other before the ceremony?" Before you make up your mind, consider the alternatives. Basically, you have three time periods for wedding photography.

Before the Ceremony

Most photographers will tell you that they not only get better pictures when they do everything beforehand, but it also relieves some of the prewedding tension. If you do everything before the service, you're more relaxed than if you take the pictures after, when you're wondering if everything is okay at the reception.

Couples tell me they enjoy the wedding and reception so much more because they aren't worried about pictures. Grooms say there's still something mystical, magical, and romantic about the moment when the bride starts her walk down the aisle, even if they've seen her before the ceremony.

The ocean at night—the lights, the fabric gently blowing in the breeze—captured on film.

(PHOTO BY MONIQUE FEIL)

Ⓞ Teddy's Tips

If you're truly not comfortable, for whatever reason, with seeing each other before the ceremony, do not let anyone—the photographer, your mother, your future mother-in-law, or the bridal consultant—talk you into going against your wishes. This is definitely up to you.

For my clients who want to take all the pictures beforehand, I find some private time for the couple to see each other in their wedding finery for the first time. I take the bride to a private room somewhere at the ceremony site and then bring in the groom. Then

I close the door and give them some private time. I've learned over the years that this time alone might be the only quality time the couple has the entire day until they get in the car to exit the reception.

Posing for pictures is work—don't let anyone tell you different. If you can build some extra time into the day for just sitting back and maybe even slipping off your wedding attire and resting for a while, it can make all the difference in the world.

Wedding Woes

Trying to finish pictures without the entire wedding party present is difficult. Be sure your wedding party knows when and where the pictures will be taken and who's expected to be photographed. Don't just assume they know what your plans are.

Before and After

Probably one of the most common ways to work in all the photos you want taken is to take some before and some after the ceremony. If you're determined not to see your partner before the wedding, this is probably the best method for getting all the shots you want.

Following the ceremony and your receiving line (if you're using one), you can do the larger pictures: the couple with the entire wedding party, the couple with the parents, and so on. It shouldn't take too long if you

After the Ceremony

You might have to take pictures following the ceremony if you choose not to see each other until after the wedding, or you might be scheduled into a church where there just isn't time to take pictures beforehand.

In most cases, the photographer should be willing to come in and do some candid shots, perhaps in the dressing room or at your home while you're adjusting your veil, or maybe take a picture of you and your mom. The bulk of your photos will be taken after the ceremony, however.

You need full cooperation from your wedding party, your parents, and anyone you want included in the photos. Be sure everyone understands that pictures will be taken immediately following the ceremony and receiving line (if you're having one).

work with the photographer. She's not a magician, so get your wedding party there on time, let them know what to expect, and smile.

A growing trend in wedding photography is placing several images on the same page like the ones you see here. Notice how they are not evenly placed as it albums of the past but scattered to give a more interesting look to the album. It truly becomes a "story" in pictures.

Photos at the Reception

Even if you have all your pictures done before or after the ceremony, some photos are "musts" *during* the reception. Again, depending on the style of the photographer, these may be posed or captured as they unfold.

These are the most common photos taken during the wedding reception:

- The couple cutting the wedding cake and feeding each other

- The toasts

- The first dance as husband and wife

- The dance with the bride's dad and the groom's mother

- The tossing of the bouquet and garter

You might ask your photographer to take other photos of special people or other special ceremonies (like your sorority sisters singing to you).

Your wedding pictures are meant to last a lifetime. When everything is over and done, they are what you have left to remember this special time. Work with the photographer to help capture the very essence of your day.

The bride and groom.

(PHOTO BY TROY HILL PHOTOGRAPHY)

"Thanks, Dad. It's been perfect."

(PHOTO BY TROY HILL PHOTOGRAPHY)

Hiring a Videographer

After you have hired a competent photographer to shoot the still pictures for your wedding, you also might want to consider booking a videographer. Videotaping by an experienced videographer can add so much life to your wedding memories that this is no longer an added "extra" but more accepted as just part of the wedding vendors.

Look at Samples

When you check out a video company, always ask to see a demo tape. This should give you an idea of the quality of work the company provides. Look for the following:

- Is there clarity both in film quality and in the coverage of events?
- Does the tape flow smoothly from one portion of the wedding to the next?
- Does the videographer use *fade-outs?*
- Is music added to the video?

Also be sure you understand whether the tape will be edited or unedited. Edited is what you would most likely prefer. Another tip: ask to see a recent tape (not just the demo that will be the best one ever shot).

Nuptial Notes

A **fade-out** is a technique where the film fades from one scene to another so the transition is smooth, giving the film a more professional feel.

Home Video Quality

The biggest complaint I hear from brides who asked Uncle Henry to tape their wedding is, "I thought it would be just like TV." Well, it's not. For a videotape to have some of the major components of a TV show, you need at least two cameras—and three would be better. Normally the videographer has several assistants helping operate the cameras.

Here are a few things you'll want to ask about:

- Is a wireless microphone available for the groom to wear to pick up the vows segment of the ceremony?

- What special effects are included, such as incorporating your baby pictures into the video or using animation?
- Will the videographer attend the rehearsal to get a feel for placement at the ceremony site and to meet the officiant?

For more help with this part of your wedding planning, turn to the "Videography Worksheet" in Appendix A.

The Package Deal

Just as you would with any other aspect of planning your wedding, ask questions about price and what's available to you:

- Can you order extra tapes or DVDs?

- Approximately how long after the wedding will you receive the DVD?

- Does the videographer use a contract? (Most do.) Is there a time limit on his contract?

- Does he charge for overtime?

- What does the videographer wear for the wedding?

Photography and videography are probably two of the most important elements with your wedding. After all, when everything is over, this is what you have left. You want your wedding memories preserved the best way possible. It's important to check out these vendors carefully so you can look back on your photos and see all the beauty and joy of the day.

Wedding Woes

Always check with the officiant to be sure you're permitted to have your ceremony videotaped. That's your responsibility, not the video company's. Nothing is more embarrassing than having the video company all set and ready to go when the officiant announces that his church or synagogue does not permit videotaping.

THE LEAST YOU NEED TO KNOW

- Be sure you feel comfortable with the photographer who will be taking your wedding pictures. You will be spending a significant amount of time together and need to have a good rapport.

- Read the photographer's contract thoroughly to understand exactly what you're paying for.

- Pictures can be taken at different stages and different time periods during the wedding day.

- Let members of your wedding party know when photographs will be taken, and ask them to be on time and to work with the photographer.

- Ask to see a demo tape of a videographer's work before you make a commitment.

JESSICA JENEEN
AND
JASON BRETT

SATURDAY, OCTOBER 15ᵀᴴ
TWO THOUSAND AND FIVE

HALF PAST FIVE IN THE EVEN

THE MA
LEXINGT

CHAPTER 11

Extra! Extra!
Read All About It!

IN THIS CHAPTER

- Selecting your invitations

- Deciding on the invitation wording

- Understanding what's included in an invitation

- Personalizing your invites with save-the-date cards, wedding newsletters, and more

- Designing a wedding program

Isn't it exciting when you open your mailbox and find a wedding invitation? You can usually tell it's for a wedding immediately—the envelope is a different size and shape from other envelopes in the pile of mail, the quality paper is usually notably nicer, and sometimes it's even a different color from that of the same old white envelopes you see in your box every day. And stand out it should—the invitation is the first hint your guests get of what your wedding will be like.

In this chapter, I tell you all about invitations, "save-the-date" cards, wedding newsletters, welcome letters, and how to create your unique wedding program.

A nice way to photograph an invitation.

(PHOTO BY FOTOBRICENO PHOTOGRAPHY)

Selecting Your Invitations

When it comes to buying your invitations, rule number 1 is: never pay full retail price for invitations. There's so much competition for your invitation order that you should never have to pay full price. You can always get something at a discount.

You can find selections for your wedding invitations at any of the following places:

- Stationery stores
- Through your bridal consultant
- Party stores
- Card/gift stores
- Bridal or tux shops
- Websites

Your wedding invitation sets the tone for the wedding and the reception to follow. It also gives the guests the first glimpse of the type and formality of your wedding. Whether it's an engraved, ivory-colored, formal invitation, or a pair of kissing frogs or two toothbrushes nestled side by side (there really are such items!), your invitation tells your guests what they can expect in terms of the mood of your big event.

You have a few things to consider when choosing your invitations—whether you want them engraved, what type of paper you like, and what size and shape you want the invitation to be. Here's a primer to give you a head start.

Nuptial Notes

A typical wedding invitation "packet" might include the invitation itself, reception card invitation, response card and return envelope (so you know who can attend), an inner envelope containing all these cards, and an outer mailing envelope.

Here's a traditional
Indian wedding invitation.

(PHOTO BY CRAIG PAUL STUDIO)

Putting Your Stamp on It

Engraved invitations are stamped with a mold (or copper plate), leaving an indentation in the paper. The ink is added to fill in the indentation, and the paper is pressed onto the plate. If you look on the back of an engraved invitation, you'll see these indentations. The copper plate is sent back to you as a keepsake.

Engraved invitations are the most formal, but they are the more expensive.

An informal invitation
issued by the couple.

A sheer overlay and ribbon decorate this formal invitation, issued by the bride's parents.

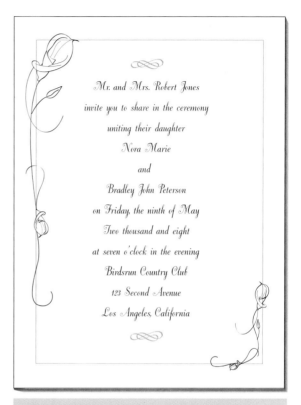

Raised floral accents make this formal invitation stand out.

Rising to the Occasion

Thermography is the most popular choice in wedding invitations. This is the opposite of engraving. In this process, the words are written out in glue, and the ink color is sprinkled over the glue. Then it's heated so the lettering is raised. Thermography is much less expensive than engraving and still has an elegant look.

The Paper Chase

The actual paper your invitation is printed on is the only item in which "what you see is what you get." It cannot be changed to another color or have the pink flowers on it made lavender (unless that's stated in the ordering process). Everything else that goes with the invitation is your choice, including...

- The color of ink(s). Companies are now offering two color inks on the same paper.

- The format. The couple's names can be enlarged or set in a different font so they stand out.

- Envelope lining.

- The wording.

Pure Poetry

Wording your wedding invitation can be a simple task, or it can be very complicated. Most invitation books (from which you will select your invitations) contain wording suggestions for almost every known circumstance (look in the front of the book). You can find everything the traditional, formal wedding invitation issued by the bride's parents, to the wording used when Uncle Fred is sending the invitations for his niece's wedding. From those samples and from the samples you see in this chapter, you should have the help you need to make the wording for your wedding invitation an easy task.

Those Little Extras

A formal wedding invitation packet should include the following:

- A reception invitation card
- A response card and self-addressed, stamped envelope
- A map with written directions

Now, Let's Party!

Most formal invitations include a reception card enclosure. Because the wedding invitation focuses on the ceremony, guests need to be instructed as to where the reception is being held. That's where reception cards come in handy.

Reception cards are enclosed with the invitation that invites the guest to the wedding reception, stating where it is and perhaps what kind of reception it is. For example, if you're having an hors-d'oeuvres-and-cocktail reception, your card may read, "Please join us following the ceremony at the country club for hors d'oeuvres and cocktails."

Wedding Woes

Never—I repeat, *never*—include a list of the stores where you're registered with your wedding invitation. You can spread the word through family and friends, but it should not go out with the invitation. You can include registry information in shower invitations, though.

Bouquet Toss

Sometimes, guests are invited only to the ceremony and not the reception. Usually, however, guests are invited to both.

Reception
immediately following ceremony
Hyatt Ballroom
123 Sparks Avenue
Carmel, Indiana

Reception card.

RSVP

RSVP is an acronym for the French phrase *répondez s'il vous plaît* and means, simply, "Please respond." When you see it written on an invitation, it means you are to call the host or return a response card by the specified date to indicate whether you can *or cannot* attend the function. The response card's matching self-addressed envelope is always stamped.

Here's one formal way to word a response card:

> *The favour of a reply is requested by April 1, 2008.*
>
> *Name* _____
>
> _____ *will attend*   _____ *will not attend*
>
> _____ *number attending*

A less formal response card could read:

> *Come join us in the celebration. Please respond by April 1, 2008.*
>
> *Name* _____
>
> _____ *will attend*   _____ *will not attend*
>
> _____ *number attending*

Mapping It Out

Map and direction cards are common in the wedding packet today because so many of your guests could be from out of town. The least-expensive way to do these cards is to print out one sheet on your PC and make copies on nice paper. You can also include hotel accommodation information, too.

Wedding Woes

Be careful about the wording on your invitation if your wedding falls around a mealtime. For clarity, list on the reception card what type of reception yours will be: "Hors D'oeuvres Reception" or "Dinner Reception." That way, guests know what type of food service to expect.

> *Please respond on or before*
> *March 15, 2008*
>
> M _____
>
> *Number of persons* _____

Response card.

Order! Order!

Order your invitations at least 4 months before the wedding, except for engraved invitations, which take much longer to produce (see the preceding section). That gives you 1 month for the order to be delivered (plenty of time) and 6 weeks for you or the calligrapher to address them. Be sure to get them in the mail 5 to 6 weeks before the wedding.

Always allow more time than you think it'll take. Just be sure everything is solidly booked with the ceremony site and the reception facility before you place your order.

When you're ready to send out your invites, take one finished invitation to the post office and have it weighed to determine the correct postage for the weight and size of your invitation. You don't want all your invitations to come back stamped in red, "Return for postage." It's not a pretty sight! For more help with ordering invitations, turn to the "Invitations Worksheet" in Appendix A.

Teddy's Tips

Always order 25 more invitations and enclosures than you think you'll need. It's much cheaper to order the extra 25 than to have to order more later.

Printed Accessories

Invitation companies offer all sorts of printed accessories to complement your wedding invitations:

Place cards are a little extra that can make your wedding more special. The place card is an individual card with the guest's name written on it and placed at that guest's place setting at the table.

Table assignment cards are usually used at large formal weddings where all the guests have been assigned a table. The card can be a single card or enclosed in an envelope. It contains the name of the guest and his or her table number.

Menu cards can be printed with the reception menu and/or the reception agenda. It's another way to spruce up your tables without going to a lot of cost. These are usually used at large formal weddings.

Place card.

Table assignment card.

Other extras you might want to include with the invitation include the following:

- Informal note cards and envelopes for general notes or as thank you notes

- Thank you cards specifically printed with the words "Thank You"

- Napkins with your names and wedding date or monogram printed on them to be used at the bar or cake tables

- Paper guest towels for the restrooms

- Personalized matches (as favors)

- Mini note pads (as favors)

By now you've covered the biggies, and the dollars are starting to add up. You still want your wedding to have uniqueness, but how can you make your wedding unique when you're on a tight budget? Read on for several inexpensive ways you can incorporate paper accents to help make your wedding unique.

Teddy's Tips

One suggestion I make to couples when ordering napkins is not to print the wedding date on them. If they're not dated, you can use the extras in your new home when entertaining.

This menu card graces the table at a reception. The gold box is a candy favor.

(PHOTO BY BROADWAY PHOTOGRAPHY)

Here's another sample of a menu card. This one also has a single rose placed in the napkin fold.

(PHOTO BY COLTER PHOTOGRAPHY

Ladies and Gentlemen, Mark Your Calendars!

"Save-the-date" cards or letters are very popular now. This can be as simple as a postcard with the couple's names, wedding date, and place; you can also do it in the form of a short letter. Its main purpose is to announce the wedding date.

Put simply, a save-the-date card might read:

> *We've finally set the date, so please put it on*
> *your calendars. We want you to be able to*
> *share this wonderful weekend with us.*
> *Saturday, May 20, 2008—New York, NY*
>
> *Sally Winters and Tom Fox*
>
>
> *(Visit our website at www.loveRus.net!)*

Let your imagination run wild, and have fun with sharing your news!

When the Masses Arrive

When guests check into the hotel, have a scaled-down copy of the weekend activities for everyone. List the following:

- Activities
- Attire for the occasion
- Time and place
- Directions
- Shuttle information
- Area activities
- City map
- A personal note from you, the couple

Just Follow Along, Please

Wedding programs make a nice addition to your wedding service. They can be simple or elaborate, but the whole purpose of the program is to enable the guests to participate in the ceremony by listing the order of the service and identifying the members of the wedding party. It's something like a theater playbill.

Other points you might add to your program include the following:

- The relationship of the wedding party member to the bride or groom (sister, brother, cousin, daughter, friend).

- Interesting information about the family. ("John and Susie are being married today on Susie's parents thirtieth wedding anniversary.")

- A note of thanks and appreciation to family.

- Your new address.

- Parts of the service that some guests might not understand.

- Wedding trivia.

- Showing respect for a departed loved one. ("The candle on the altar is in memory of John's father.")

- Names of other participants in the wedding ceremony (readers, greeters, soloists, musicians, guest book attendant).

Keep It Simple … or Go to Extremes!

Programs can be as simple as a single sheet of colored paper printed on a computer and duplicated. Roll it up and tie it with a coordinating ribbon, and you have a simple, attractive, and inexpensive presentation. For an elaborate look, print your programs on several sheets of paper covered with a heavy outer paper, emboss or engrave monograms on the front, and then tie the paper with coordinating ribbons.

One of the most elaborate wedding programs is a missal. This includes, verbatim, everything the priest, rabbi, or officiant says. This type of program is especially nice when the majority of your guests are not of your faith. This type of program is more costly simply because of its length, but you still can produce it economically.

Wedding programs are used more today than in the past. They are just another way of treating your guests with a little extra care and making them feel right at home. For help with wedding programs, turn to the "Program Worksheet" in Appendix A.

These programs were a special touch with floral paper and pretty pink ribbon.

(PHOTO BY EMILY'S IMAGES)

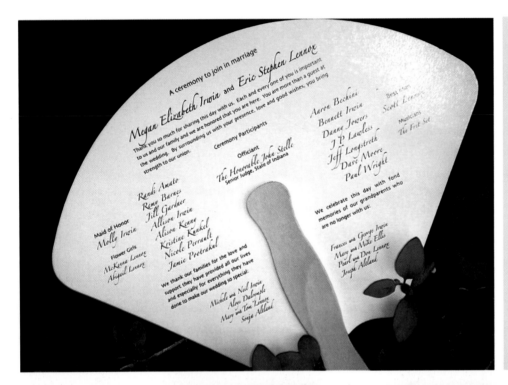

This fan-shaped program came in handy at an outdoor wedding.

(PHOTO BY IRWIN)

At this wedding, guests were asked to write a message to the couple instead of signing a guest book.

(PHOTO BY FOTOBRICENO PHOTOGRAPHY)

A new way to do a guest book: have your guests sign the mat around a picture frame.

(PHOTO BY WYANT PHOTOGRAPHY)

THE LEAST YOU NEED TO KNOW

- Always ask about getting a discount on invitations; you should never pay full price. Always order 25 more invitations than you think you'll need.

- Consider sending a save-the-date card if your guests are scattered across the country and you think an advance notice would help.

- Think about incorporating a wedding program into your ceremony.

CHAPTER 12

Do Yourself
a Favor

IN THIS CHAPTER

- Showing you care with favors
- Getting lots of ideas for favors, from simple to sensational
- Choosing gifts for your attendants
- Creating a unique "welcome basket"

In this chapter, I talk about the use of favors at your wedding. I offer some advice on ideas to use for favors and how to create your own ideas. I also talk about what to give your wedding party members as thank you gifts.

I also share some wonderful ways to incorporate welcome baskets (even on a tight budget) into your wedding package. Read on, and let your imagination run wild.

Favoring Your Friends

Favors—those little gifts you give your guests as a thank you for attending your wedding—are a big trend. You can select expensive and elaborate favors or very inexpensive and simple favors. The idea is not to dazzle your guests with great favors, but to make them feel special and appreciated and to add a special touch to your wedding. (For help in planning favors, use the "Favors Worksheet" in Appendix A.)

Here's a pretty party favor all tied with ribbon. Wonder what's inside?

(PHOTO BY MONIQUE FEIL)

Godiva chocolate is always a crowd-pleaser.

(PHOTO BY MONIQUE FEIL)

Wedding Woes

Be sure you have plenty of favors to go around. Nothing would be worse than having more guests than favors and having to decide who gets one and who doesn't!

Some favors are more expensive than others, but the bottom line of making your guests feel special is what counts. Some favors can be personalized or imprinted with names and dates; either the company where you purchase the products or your local printer can probably do this for you.

Look over the following ideas for favors, and see what other ideas you can come up with:

- Candy—in either an elegant box tied with ribbon or a cloth bag tied with ribbon or cording

- Candy bar imprinted with "Thank you for sharing our day"

A gold favor piece of chocolate. Always popular.

(PHOTO BY MELANIE MAUER)

The ever-popular candy bar. This is from a country wedding.

(PHOTO BY IRWIN)

And this is the back of the candy bar. Love the tractor!

(PHOTO BY IRWIN)

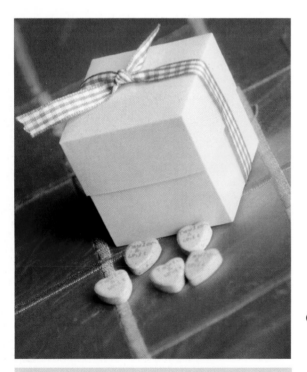

Pink candy favor boxes—too pretty to open!

(PHOTO BY MELANIE MAUER)

- Individual small candles at each place setting

- Golf tees or golf balls imprinted with the couple's names

- A single silk or fresh flower, tied with a ribbon, at each female place setting

- A bottle of bubbles to blow as the bride and groom dance their first dance

- A small tulle bag or paper cone filled with rose petals or potpourri

- A scroll paper printed with your favorite verse or poem

Wedding Woes

When ordering candy through the mail, be sure you know when it will be delivered so you can arrange for someone to be at home to receive it. What an ugly mess it would be to find 300 chocolate bars melted all over your front porch because no one was there to accept the package. Not a pretty sight!

- Water bottles imprinted with the couple's names

- A huge glass jar filled with individually wrapped cookies and a note that reads "Sweet Dreams" (Guests take a cookie as they leave the reception.)

- A CD of the couple's favorite songs with their picture on the jacket covers (These can be wrapped in the wedding colors to add to the table décor.)

- Individual splits of wine or champagne with the couple's picture on the bottle

- A printed card at each place letting guests know that a donation to a favorite charity was made in their honor

- Sun block wrapped in bright paper for summer weddings

- Beach balls imprinted with the couple's names

- Candy corn in small natural baskets for autumn weddings

- Key chains imprinted with the couple's names

- Music boxes

- Gourmet jellybeans or mixed nuts in a decorative jar or canister

- Beer mugs or wine glasses etched with the couple's names

- Flower bulbs wrapped in spring shades of tulle

- Pears wrapped together with a small sign "The Perfect Pair"

- Packets of flower seeds imprinted with the couple's names

- Blank journals

This couple chose to leave all kinds of individually wrapped cookies by the exit for guests to take.

(PHOTO BY COLTER PHOTOGRAPHY)

Of all favor choices, this one is probably my favorite. The paper reads that a donation has been made to the American Cancer Society in lieu of favors and in memory of someone special. What a great way to spend favor money.

(PHOTO BY THE WEDDING CASA)

- Imprinted note pads or matchbooks

- Tennis balls, visors, or other sports items imprinted with the couple's names

- Small picture frames

- Holiday ornaments or small Christmas wreaths for a December wedding

- Small wicker baskets (check out some of the wholesale houses) with an arrangement of silk flowers, assorted candies, or decorative soaps tucked inside

- Heart-shape items or items that feature hearts on them, such as magnets, mugs, or candies (ideal for a Valentine's Day wedding)

- Small sombreros or piñatas for a Mexican-themed wedding, or floral leis for a Hawaiian-themed wedding

Teddy's Tips

Cluster your favors to make the table centerpiece. For example, small individual pots with flowers or plants arranged in a circle in the center of the table make a lovely focal point. You can even drape some tulle around the base of the circle or tie some ribbons around the pots. As guests leave, ask that they each take a pot with them.

Here, the candles serve as place cards. Names are printed on the candles and set at each place.

(PHOTO BY FOTOBRICENO)

Little umbrellas to keep the heat or rain away.

(PHOTO BY MELANIE MAUER

This is a popular favor: jars with all kinds of candy await the guests, who fill their own bags.

(PHOTO BY MELANIE MAUER)

An example of a gift basket to be left for guests at their hotel. This couple chose items made in Indiana for their basket; their guests came from all over the country.

(PHOTO BY IRWIN)

Attending to Your Attendants

The gifts you choose to give to your attendants (a nice way of saying, "Thanks for putting up with my irrational behavior for the past six months") need to be custom-designed for your wedding party. I'm not saying go out and have something custom-designed for each and every member of your wedding party. I just mean you should try to make the gift truly special.

Think about who they are and what they like. Nothing is carved in stone that says you must buy every bridesmaid and every groomsman the same thing. I know that's usually easier, but with a little planning, you can come up with some unique gift ideas for these special friends.

Welcome One and All!

With our society so scattered and family and friends all over the world, weddings have become more than just a way to spend a couple hours on a Saturday afternoon. With that in mind, the idea of the welcome basket was born. Because guests come from all over, it's nice to offer them some goodies when they check into the hotel.

Welcome baskets or packages can come in all sizes and shapes. Even the tightest budget can accommodate a welcome basket for a few family members. A lot of "baskets" are really fancy bags (you know, the colorful kind you can find in craft stores). You can fill them with anything you want, but here are some items you should include:

- A note from the couple

- An itinerary of the weekend

- A map showing the ceremony and reception sites

- Emergency phone numbers

- A small gift item, usually something to eat

- Something regional, like coffee if your wedding is in the northwest; cheese and crackers if the wedding is in Wisconsin; or Hershey Kisses if the wedding is in Hershey, Pennsylvania

- Bottled water

- Wine or sparkling grape juice

Welcome baskets or bags, however simple or elaborate, are just a delightful way to say, "We're glad you're here! Have a great weekend!"

THE LEAST YOU NEED TO KNOW

- Say thank you to your guests for helping make your day so special by presenting them with favors.

- Favors don't have to be expensive; something as simple as Hershey Kisses wrapped in pretty fabric and tied with a ribbon can be a nice touch.

- Try to choose gifts for your attendants that have some special or personal meaning. If possible, have the gifts personalized.

- If your budget will allow, try to have a welcome basket waiting at the hotel for out-of-town guests.

Rose Petal

nd–Off

Clos

(PHOTO BY MELANIE MAUER)

CHAPTER 13

Let the Party Begin!

IN THIS CHAPTER

- Planning your reception agenda: when to do what
- Handling wedding gifts at the reception
- Making your grand exit

The ceremony is over. You can breathe a little easier. Now, prepare to be the guests of honor at one of the greatest parties you've ever attended!

Whether you're having a small, intimate celebration with family and a few close friends, or the party of the century with dinner and dancing until dawn, you and your spouse will want to enjoy it. Let others do the worrying for now. This is a time to concentrate on your new spouse and your friends and family who have come from all over to share this day with you. The best way to do that is to have certain things decided ahead of time and to make all who need to know aware of the schedule.

Activities to Include

What happens when you arrive at the reception? Should there be some kind of order to the events? Can you just mingle and do things as the spirit moves you? The answers are both yes and no.

Remember that this is your reception. The agenda needs to be of your choosing, not what Cousin Sarah says a reception is supposed to include. Discuss your options and what you want to see happen at the reception. For example, do you want your guests to be welcomed with a glass of champagne? When is the best man going to make his toast? Do you want to throw a bouquet and garter? Do you want a rigid dance order that specifies who dances with whom and when? Setting an agenda helps determine how the activities flow.

Notice how everything on the table is coordinated, from the tan linens to glasses edged in gold. A flower is placed in each napkin.

(PHOTO BY CRAIG PAUL STUDIO)

This long table is set with lots of candlelight and menu cards placed inside the napkin folds. An elegant look.

(PHOTO BY BRAD BASKER)

The sweetheart table, set just for two. Notice the embroidered monograms on the fabric runners.

(PHOTO BY EMILY'S IMAGES)

This is another nice idea for the reception. Guests are asked to write a note to the couple, which will be placed in their scrapbook.

(PHOTO BY GARBO PRODUCTIONS)

This is the aftermath of a game played at some receptions. After all the toasts are made, sometimes the best man stands up and very seriously asks that all women in the room who have a key to the groom's apartment please turn them in. It can be very funny, especially when an elderly aunt or grandma drops her key on the table.

(PHOTO BY RAAB)

Call it whatever you like, but even an informal, family-only reception should have some kind of an agenda. For your agenda to be carried out, you need someone to help move the events along. This is another place where an experienced bridal consultant can be invaluable.

Greeting Your Guests

Whether to have a receiving line is a decision based on several factors. If you've taken all your pictures before the wedding, you can easily receive guests after the ceremony and move on to the reception. If you haven't taken all the photos, you have to decide if you want to take more time to do the receiving line. A normal receiving line with the couple and both sets of parents receiving 200 guests will

This couple displayed several of their favorite photos, including one of their four-legged friend.

(PHOTO BY THE WEDDING CASA)

take approximately 30 to 45 minutes. Add to that another 30 to 45 minutes for the photographer to finish taking pictures, and you've added 1½ hours to the time after the wedding.

If you have more than 200 guests, consider other options for greeting your guests. Perhaps you and your spouse could move from table to table at the reception greeting guests instead. Another idea is for the couple to come back into the ceremony site and release the rows as the ushers might do. The bottom line is that your guests expect to be able to say hello to you on your wedding day. They almost feel rejected if time is not built into the schedule for them to wish you the best.

A Big Hand for Mr. and Mrs. …

Many couples want to be introduced as they arrive at the reception. Ask your band or DJ to do the honors if you aren't using a master of ceremonies (MC) for the evening. Most are happy to assist. Consider whether you want your entire wedding party to be announced or just you, the couple.

Teddy's Tips

Here is a great opportunity to make a relative or close friend feel very special: instead of relying on a master of ceremonies, disc jockey, or bandleader to make the introductions, why not have someone you know (and who knows the guests and can pronounce their names!) handle this task? Obviously, it should be someone who can stand up in front of a crowd and speak without tripping over his or her tongue!

Introducing Mr. and Mrs.—usually the first formal part of the reception.

(PHOTO BY WYANT PHOTOGRAPHY)

Raise Your Glasses

When you're finished eating, you might want to schedule a toast or two. Traditionally, the best man offers the first toast of the evening. He stands, gets the guests' attention, and makes a toast to the new couple. The toast should be simple and sincere. The groom then should thank him and offer a toast to his new bride. After that, it's an open floor—anyone can offer a toast, or it can stop there.

When a toast is proposed, all should rise—except the person or persons who are being toasted. Both the bride and groom would remain seated for the best man's toast. For the groom's toast, only the bride would be seated.

Bouquet Toss

As with many of the wedding traditions we observe today, the cake cutting dates to ancient times. In ancient Rome, the couple would share a hard biscuit, each taking a bite from it. The wedding officiant would then crumble the remaining portion over the couple's heads. This was thought to bring bounty to the couple, good luck, and many children. Guests at these ancient weddings would rush to the site where the biscuit was crumbled to obtain any leftover crumbs for their own good luck. Over the centuries, this cake crumbling has evolved into modern wedding guests having a piece of cake at the reception or taking a piece home with them.

Cutting the Cake

Following the toast, and depending on what you've decided to do, you can go right into cutting the cake. This is another place you will want formal photographs, so be sure your photographer knows the order of events.

Have a plate and napkin ready at the table to place the cake on and to wipe your sticky fingers. Then take turns feeding each other a small piece of cake. Notice the word *small*. I find it very interesting when a couple gets into a food

Bouquet Toss

The term *toasting* dates back to the sixteenth century. Those attending a function placed a spice-laden crouton in the bottom of a wine glass. This was either for flavor or nourishment—who knows? The last person to drink from the glass and find the toast not only claimed it, but was given good wishes.

Cake-cutting time. This couple takes the first slice on their cake. Notice how their hands are joined together to make the first cut.

(PHOTO BY GARBO PRODUCTIONS)

Their first dance as husband and wife.

(PHOTO BY WYANT PHOTOGRAPHY)

fight while they're feeding each other the cake. This is supposed to be a tender moment, symbolic of your union and the life you will share.

Get Your Dancing Cards Ready

If your reception includes dancing, it can begin following the cake ceremony. The bride and groom are the first to dance at the reception, and some couples choose a favorite song for that first dance. The bride and groom can dance the entire first dance, or the bride's father can cut in and finish that first dance with his daughter. Some brides request the first dance with their groom and the entire second dance with their father.

Some popular songs for the dance with Dad are "Daddy's Little Girl," "Sunrise, Sunset," and "Butterfly Kisses." (Check with your local music store for sheet music if the band or DJ doesn't have the song you would like played.)

When you have the first dance or two out of the way, it's time to let loose and get the party moving. This is where the homework you did before you chose your DJ or band should pay off. If your dance floor is filled with dancers most of the night, you get an A for all your advance work.

It's a Toss-Up

Later in the reception, if you choose, the bride can throw the bouquet and garter. Here again, you'll need help to make the announcement. Ask for all single women to join the bride on the dance floor. It's customary for the bride to turn her back to the single women and, after a countdown, toss the bouquet. Tradition has it that the woman who catches the bouquet will be the next to marry.

Teddy's Tips

If your guests signed the guest book at the ceremony, there's no need to have it at the reception, although you might want to have it available for latecomers who didn't get a chance to sign it earlier.

Wedding Woes

Don't make the dancing segment of the wedding so complicated that the cast needs cue cards to tell who's dancing with whom and to what song. I normally recommend no more than two or three special dances.

Hands up, ladies! Here comes the bouquet!
(PHOTO BY EMILY'S IMAGES)

Now it's the groom's turn. Instead of using a chair to sit on while the groom removes your garter, why not ask the best man to kneel on one knee so you can sit on his leg? It makes for a great picture and is certainly warmer than a cold chair. Sometimes, the band or DJ provides a drum roll here and then plays "The Stripper" for the actual garter removal.

When the groom has the garter in hand, he moves off the dance floor and, with his back to his single male friends, tosses the garter. Again, the man who catches the garter will be the next to marry.

Yes, he did take off the garter with his teeth!

(PHOTO BY WYANT PHOTOGRAPHY)

What Else?

You might want to incorporate other traditions or ceremonies into your wedding reception. Perhaps you'd like some religious customs or prayers recited (such as the prayers over the wine and bread at a Jewish wedding). Some sororities and fraternities have rituals they perform during the evening. Maybe there's someone you want to honor with a special dance. This is your reception—make it personal.

The end of their first dance. The bride's facial expression says it all.

(PHOTO BY RAAB)

Always try to include your heritage in your wedding. At this wedding the friends of the bride and groom are lifting them in chairs as part of a celebratory dance, a Jewish tradition.

(PHOTO BY WYANT PHOTOGRAPHY)

Making Your Getaway

The time has come, my dears, to make your grand exit. You and your groom need to decide when you want to leave your wedding reception. Most of the couples I work with want to stay for the whole reception. After all, it's a party for you, given in your honor. These couples don't want to miss anything: the fun, the music, the dancing, and talking with friends and family members they've not seen for months. So if that's what you'd like to do, go for it.

Give your parents a hug, and thank them for this wonderful day and for all their support. Do the same with your new parents-in-law. Then, make your exit. If you have petals you want guests to toss as you make your mad dash to the waiting car, have one of your bridesmaids gather guests by the exit and pass out the petals. The showering simply means good luck and, according to legend, also promotes fertility.

The photographer will want to capture this moment on film. Give her time to get set up and then run—do not walk—to the car and wave good-bye. Now, you're off. You're alone for the first time since earlier that day, or maybe even the previous day. It's now your time to enjoy each other, relax, and have a great honeymoon!

Wedding Woes

One bride lost a $100 deposit when a guest, not knowing the rules, passed out birdseed to the guests to toss. The church claimed the deposit as a cleanup fee. So check with facility beforehand!

A grand exit with sparklers!

(PHOTO BY MELANIE MAUER PHOTOGRAPHY)

THE LEAST YOU NEED TO KNOW

- Plan a reception agenda so the reception has a continual flow and the photographer can be ready for each activity—but don't feel you have to incorporate any or all customs into your reception.

- Have the reception manager place a table for gifts in the main room of the reception, and ask a friend to direct guests bearing presents to this table.

- When it's time for you to leave the reception, be sure to say goodbye to your parents and your new in-laws. They've worked hard on this wedding and would probably appreciate being thanked.

CHAPTER 14

Making the Most
of Your Dollars

IN THIS CHAPTER

- Stretching your wedding dollars
- Saving on flowers, music, photography, and more
- Trimming reception costs
- Understanding contracts and agreements

I've talked about budgets (I know—still not your favorite subject), and I've discussed questions to ask vendors to be sure you're getting what you pay for. In this chapter, let's get some serious work done and trim up that budget (in ways no one will recognize) and talk a little about contracts and agreements (I know, I know, more of that boring stuff, but nonetheless, very important). Keep in mind the wise wedding consumer's thoughts: a wedding is a product you are purchasing (don't take me literally on that—but you do purchase flowers, invitations, church rental—you know what I mean). You need to focus on where you are spending your dollars.

"Think before you spend" is a wise statement to keep in mind as you plan your wedding. But don't worry—there are lots of ways to cut costs and still have the wedding of your dreams!

Prioritizing Your Pennies

In previous chapters, I suggested some questions for you to ask the vendors you're considering using. I told you what to expect from these vendors, and you started spending some of those precious wedding budget dollars. Before you blink and all those dollars have disappeared, let's look at ways you can trim some costs from your wedding bill.

Smart wedding shopping techniques begin with having patience and not being an impulsive buyer. Time is your friend when you're in the wedding market. As you shop with the various vendors, give yourself the time you need to be sure you're getting the best product for the best price.

A boat is the site for this reception. The tables are set simply with greens, Gerber daisies, and large pillar candles all nestled down the center.

(PHOTO BY MONIQUE FEIL)

A lot depends on the importance you place on each area of the wedding. If a certain photographer is very important to you, figure out a way to incorporate his fee into your plans.

The following sections give you some ideas of specific ways you can cut wedding expenses and stretch your wedding dollars.

Teddy's Tips

Don't ever be afraid to ask if an item can be discounted or rented or if a vendor can do something less expensively. What more can someone say than "No"? Many times, you'll find yourself pleasantly surprised by the answer.

Finding Ways to Cut Your Floral Bill

There are several ways to cut costs in the floral department:

Check with the church to see if another wedding is scheduled on the same day as yours. If so, ask the other couple about sharing the expense for ceremony site flowers.

At the ceremony, have the pew markers designed to double as centerpieces at the reception. This takes some coordination between the florist and reception facility, but I've had several brides use this cost-cutting technique.

If you live in a large metropolitan area, check to see if there's a local floral design school. Many times, students at these trade schools will gladly produce your wedding flowers for the cost of materials so they can gain experience and a letter of recommendation.

Use balloons or fabrics instead of flowers or greenery to cover blemishes on the walls (exposed pipes, marks,

etc.). The balloons are cheaper, cover more, add a festive party look, and can be assembled the morning of the wedding.

Select locally grown flowers.

Use only flowers in season.

Instead of carrying a bouquet of roses, you can carry a single rose or a small floral arrangement on a family Bible or prayer book.

Use lots of greenery (ferns, plants, palms) mixed with votive candles for a soft, lush, less-expensive way to add some décor to the church.

Check with your florist or a party rental store about the possibility of renting centerpieces.

Place small vases on the head table, and place the bridesmaids' bouquets in them to add color to the table.

This table is simply decorated with lots of greenery and Gerber daisies down the center. Gerber daisies are wonderful for adding bright color here and there, and they're an inexpensive flower.

(PHOTO BY MONIQUE FEIL)

This pew marker will double as the centerpiece for a table at the reception.

(PHOTO FROM THE AUTHOR'S COLLECTION)

The entrance to this home wedding has been spruced up with sunflowers and grapevine. In the background, you can see the guest book table.

(PHOTO BY THE WEDDING CASA)

Dressing for Less

If you're a very talented sewer or have access to a good seamstress, make your gown and veil. You can save some big bucks here. Some other ideas for trimming your budget in this area include the following:

Check out the bridal discount stores, but be very careful! If you can buy a dress off the rack at one of these stores, you probably will come away with a bargain. If the store must order a gown for you, be sure you understand the terms completely.

Look for a ready-to-wear tea-length gown that requires very little alteration.

Look for sales at the bridal shops. You can often find truly lovely gowns on the sale rack for one third to one half off the original price.

Wedding Woes

All bridal discount stores are not created equal. Try to buy off the rack, because ordering from these establishments can be risky. Before you put down a deposit, be sure you understand what you're buying and what the store will do about flaws or mistakes.

Check out the "gently used" dress shops. These gowns have been worn maybe once, some not at all, and are a small fraction of what you would pay for a new gown.

Consider wearing your mother's or even your grandmother's gown (see Chapter 8). Many times, gowns from days gone by are actually back in style or will blend with the theme of your wedding.

Order your bridesmaids' dresses from national catalogs. One bride ordered all seven of her bridesmaids' gowns from a catalog and saved half of what she would have paid in a shop.

Rent your gown and your bridesmaids' dresses. This is a great idea when you don't have a lot of time to plan your wedding. Some bridal shops even rent gowns. Check before you visit.

Borrow shoes from a friend, or buy inexpensive ballet slippers. In my wedding, I wore white slippers that cost only $6.95, and no one knew the difference.

Always look for package tuxedos deals, such as, "Rent five, get the groom's tux free." (See Chapter 8 for more on outfitting the groom and groomsmen.)

Try to rent the tuxedos from stores that have a local warehouse. Then if you run into problems, you stand a much better chance of getting the problem resolved.

By taking some time to think carefully about what's

Teddy's Tips

If you're a craftsy person, why not buy a plain pair of slippers and decorate them yourself? Use sequins, pearls, buttons, or whatever you like to design a unique pair of slippers at a fraction of the cost of buying a pair.

important to you and your groom, you can prioritize those items where you want to spend the bucks. And as I've shown already, there are many ways to trim dollars from your expense sheet to make the best use of your wedding bucks!

Regulating Your Reception Expenses

Here are some tips to help trim reception costs:

Plan your reception for some other time than mealtime. You can save quite a bit of money by having a morning or early afternoon wedding and reception.

Watch for sales on liquor or paper goods. Ask about discounts when buying by the case.

Use paper products instead of renting crystal or china.

Use carafes of wine on the tables rather than bottles. Open wine bottles can be wasted, specially if the guests at a table don't drink alcohol.

Rent a champagne fountain instead of using champagne bottles on the tables, or have individual glasses of champagne served to guests.

Using cheese and fruit with some crackers and different kinds of snack breads is an inexpensive way to stretch your food dollars.

(PHOTO BY MONIQUE FEIL)

Instead of offering an open bar, limit your guests' choices to only wine and/or beer, or serve a champagne punch instead of other liquor (see Chapter 7 for more about your options when serving liquor).

Use only house brands of liquor. Most of your guests wont' notice, and the cost difference between house brands and premiums is tremendous.

Check local vocational schools for students or recent graduates in food service or decorating who would be willing to produce the food or decorations for your reception in exchange for the experience and the exposure. Many times, those just starting out will offer their services at a discount for a reference. You gotta start somewhere!

Cut down the size of your guest list. Remember, the cost of the reception equals about 40 to 45 percent of your total budget. If you can't feed a crowd of 500 a sit-down dinner, try to cut that number to what you can handle. You can even do two receptions. Immediately following the service, have the cake and punch at the church social hall for the larger crowd. Then, later that day, offer your close friends and family the dinner-and-dancing reception.

If you're having a do-it-yourself reception, accept all the offers you can from family and friends who volunteer to bring in items. This can be risky—someone might not follow through on a promise (it happens)—but it can save you many dollars.

Borrow as many items as you can. Don't rent or buy a brand-new punch bowl, cake servers, or toasting glasses. Some friend or family member who has married recently might have these items. Ask to borrow them.

If you need extra help with serving, check with a local sorority or fraternity. Many times, for a donation to their philanthropy project, these groups will send several people to help serve your reception.

Managing Your Music Dollars

Music can add some large expenses to your wedding, but if you do your homework, you can save money:

- Check into using local high school or college student musicians instead of paying more for experienced musicians. Be sure to listen to them perform so you know what you are hiring. Like any other musical vendor, be sure they understand what they're expected to wear and how long you need them to play.

- Ask a reliable friend who has some experience and understanding of what makes a good DJ to play some CDs for you at the reception. He'll need a good sound system.

- Hire the musicians for a minimum amount of time.

Economizing on the Extras

Borrow any items you can. Don't buy a ring bearer's pillow, cake servers, or toasting glasses. Unless you get these items as gifts, there's little reason to spend extra money on something you'll use only once.

Here are a few more simple ways to trim costs:

- Don't have a date stamped on your wedding napkins. That way, you can use the extras in your new home after the wedding.

- Have the ring pillow made or make it yourself. It's fairly simple and will mean even more to you.

- Make your favors and/or your attendants gifts (see Chapter 12).

- Buy things as you have the cash for them. For example, buy stamps for the invitations a couple packs at a time.

- Get the families involved. You'd be surprised what talents are out there.

Bouquet Toss

One bride asked her grandmother to make some of the extras for her wedding, which made the grandmother feel so much more a part of the planning. She made the ring bearer's pillow, the bride's two garters (one to throw, one to keep), crocheted hankies for each bridesmaid to carry, and a table cover for the cake table with the couple's initials embroidered on it.

Using items you have around the house can help with decorating.

(PHOTO BY MONIQUE FEIL)

Paring Photography Costs

Photography is such an important part of the wedding festivities, and you want good photographs you can enjoy for years to come. Fortunately, you can trim some of these costs:

- Hire a professional photographer to shoot the formal wedding pictures (see Chapter 10) and then have a trusted friend who has some skill with a camera take the candid shots at the reception.

- Check out colleges and trade schools for an advanced photography student to shoot your wedding for a set fee and then give you the negatives for processing.

Cutting Costs on Invitations

You can save money on invitations by including the reception information on the invitation instead of on a separate card. You can also save money by using a postcard for the response card. The card costs about the same as an enclosure card and envelope but you'll save on postage.

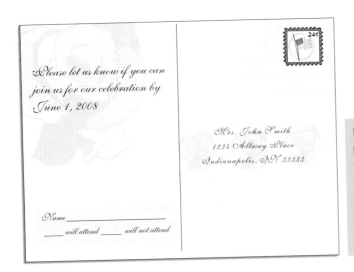

It's perfectly acceptable to send guests a prestamped, postcard-size response card with which to reply to your wedding. The cost to print these is about the same as an enclosure and envelope, but the big savings is in the postage, as it's less expensive to mail postcards than envelopes.

Contracts and Agreements

During the course of your wedding planning, you'll most likely be required to sign several contracts or agreements with the various vendors you're hiring.

If you're not accustomed to a contract and its terminology, take someone with you who is familiar with the legal mumbo jumbo.

Most contracts are written by an attorney who wasn't hired to make legal jargon understandable to the uninitiated. If you aren't sure what the contract means, if you need a point clarified, or if you want to be sure you understand what's required of you, ask the vendor to explain the contract in lay terms. If you're still not sure what it means, ask to take the contract out of the store to share with your family, your attorney, or someone else who can help you. Most vendors don't have a problem letting you take the contract—if they do, maybe you should wonder why. The contract is for both your protection and that of the vendor's. Although it can be confusing, it does have a legitimate purpose during the wedding planning.

If you use musicians from local schools, you might not have contracts with them. A letter of agreement from the sponsor of the student string quartet, for example, would do the trick. With the floral schools, maybe you'll have a letter of what's expected and the supplies needed to complete the task.

Always keep your contracts in a safe, easily accessible place. When you need to look at your contracts, you won't want to spend hours trying to find them.

Wedding Woes

Never—I repeat, *never*—sign anything, whether it's a contract, agreement, or letter of intent, if you do not completely understand its meaning.

THE LEAST YOU NEED TO KNOW

- Cutting costs from your wedding budget is easier than you might think.

- When it comes to stretching your wedding dollars, think creatively.

- Never be afraid to ask for discounts or to inquire about renting items instead of buying them.

- Always be sure you understand what you're signing when you put your signature on a contract or agreement. If you don't understand the document, find someone who can explain it to you before you sign on the dotted line.

PART 4

Circling the Wagons:
Preparing for the Main Event

IN THIS PART

15 And in This Corner …

16 I Think I'm Losing My Mind!

17 Much Ado About Everything: Prenuptial Preparation

Even if you're already well into planning your wedding, I recommend you read Part 4 from start to finish. It can make all the difference in your emotional state for the remainder of your planning. If you've turned to this part before you've begun any actual planning, you're taking a good first step toward having as stress-free a wedding as possible.

In this part, you learn what goes on emotionally—and mostly subconsciously—with some of the people around you as the process of planning a wedding unfolds. I discuss marriage as a rite of passage and why some decisions are so emotional for those involved. I also offer some practical tips that might help smooth things over. I tell you how to deal with wedding stress, how to work with divorced parents and blended families, where you can turn for help, and what you can do to help yourself. So strap yourself in tight, and get ready for the roller-coaster ride!

CHAPTER 15

And in This
Corner ...

IN THIS CHAPTER

- Understanding marriage as a rite of passage
- Knowing what to expect emotionally
- Winning the power struggle
- Dealing with tension between parents
- Keeping your sanity

A marriage can be a very stressful event even under the best of circumstances. Understanding what goes on emotionally during this process can help curtail unnecessary emotional turmoil from invading your wedding bliss.

In this chapter and the next, I share with you why planning a wedding can be such a stressful time, and give you some stress-busting strategies to help you relax and enjoy the process—and keep the peace in your families!

The Emotional Roller Coaster— What to Expect

Marriage is a rite of passage. You're passing from one part of your life into a new part; you're leaving the primary role of child and taking on the new role of spouse. This universal rite demonstrates to a community that one of its own is old enough, responsible enough, and mature enough to take a mate.

There are three basic rites of passage: birth, marriage, and death. Of these three, marriage is the only one you choose. With this rite of passage comes a whole slew of emotions. These emotions are what fuel that roller-coaster ride you and your mother—and perhaps other members of the family—find yourselves on during the planning process.

Let's talk about your emotions for a minute. Keep in mind that most of what goes on with your emotions during this time is subconscious. You don't know why you feel the way you do; it's just how you feel. Right now you're engaged to a wonderful person. You're excited, you're scared, you're happy, you worry about how well your in-laws will like you, you wonder whether your parents will get along—all kinds of thoughts are running through your head. Now throw in the fact that your mother insists on beef for the entrée and that you and your fiancé both want chicken, or that she thinks pink is a terrible color for the bridesmaids' dresses while you've had your heart set on pink for years.

You have the makings for some major fireworks, but what's really going on here? Is it about beef and chicken? Is it about the 10 different shades of pink you want to incorporate? I doubt it. It's about the bonds between parent and child, it's about power and control, and it's about growing up.

Mother and Me

At this point in your life, you may be torn between yearning for independence and yet not being ready to leave the nest. You want to make your own choices and decisions, but you might be reluctant to give up the security of having someone take care of you. Even if you've been out on your own for a number of years, you're still your mother's child.

Your mother also might be feeling torn. She has reared you to be an independent person, but she's not really ready to lose her baby. She wants you to be strong, but she wants to be sure you make the right decisions (which often translates into the decisions she would make). Your mother is afraid that the marriage will break the bonds between the two of you, and that makes her sad. So while she might be perfectly willing to argue over beef or chicken or your choice of colors, you can be fairly certain that's not really what she's upset about. She's afraid the marriage will change your relationship with her. She's afraid your new spouse will replace her and you won't need her anymore.

A kiss for the bride from her proud father as mom looks on.

(PHOTO BY FOTOBRICENO)

She's also afraid of the aging process—you getting married means she's getting older. Again, she's afraid of losing her baby. She's afraid of many things, most of which she can't explain to you, nor does she understand.

Don't be too hard on Mom. Try not to let these subconscious emotional issues get in the way of your planning, fun, and excitement.

Teddy's Tips

For more insights on being the mother of the bride, check out *The Pocket Idiot's Guide to Being the Mother of the Bride* by Amy Zavatto (Alpha Books, 2005).

Bouquet Toss

One bride I worked with found her mother pulling away rather than becoming overly involved in the wedding plans. This was partly because the mother had read so many articles and heard so many complaints about overbearing mothers taking over the wedding that she went overboard the opposite way. Many times, she didn't offer any opinions and only said "That's nice, dear," when told about details. She offered little help with any of the plans. The mother never even discussed anything besides a general dollar figure, so the bride ended up feeling like her mother couldn't have cared less that her daughter was getting married. In reality, the mother was trying too hard to let her daughter make her own decisions.

Daddy's Little Girl

Much is written about the prewedding tension between mother and daughter. But what about daughter and Dad? Where does he fit into the plan?

Fathers are generally very interesting creatures when it comes to making plans for their daughter's big day. Your dad is proud of the woman you've become, and he wants only the very best for you. On the other hand, he may be somewhat jealous of your groom, the man who is going to take you away. Dad has been your protector; now he's giving up that role, and he does so with a little sadness. It doesn't matter how he feels about your groom; his little girl is growing up. And here, too, it doesn't matter if you're a 30-year-old bride or a 22-year-old bride, you are still Daddy's little girl.

Dad also might feel left out of all the planning stages. At times, it does seem like a solely mother-daughter planning frenzy—kind of like a marathon of planning. If he seems grumpy or on edge from time to time, he might just want to be part of the process, too (other than writer of the checks), but he just doesn't know how to ask. When you ask if he would like to help, he may gruffly tell you that you and your mother are doing just fine with the planning, but he might not tell you that he feels better just that you had extended the offer.

Ask your dad how, or if, he wants to be involved in the wedding planning. If he gives the go-ahead, offer him some task that he will feel comfortable handling.

Always try to keep your dad informed about the decisions you've made. Try to ask his advice and counsel. This will make him feel close to you and needed.

A dance with her dad as the groom and his mom wait their turn.

(PHOTO BY COLTER PHOTOGRAPHY)

Teddy's Tips

Pick up a copy of Jennifer Lata Rung's *The Pocket Idiot's Guide to Being the Father of the Bride*, now in its Second Edition (Alpha Books, 2006) to help Dad through all the wedding planning steps and down the aisle.

Mama's Baby Boy

So you think this chapter is just for the bride and her family? Well, as a former mother of the groom and one more to go, I'm here to tell you that the emotional stress happens to the males, too. While it has always been associated with the female gender, grooms, along with their fathers, and of course, the mothers, all go through the same rite of passage as the bride and her family.

The best advice I can offer grooms is to get involved with the wedding plans (it's your wedding, too) and keep those lines of communication open with your family. You and your family are also experiencing the same emotions as your bride and her family. But because you're the man, it's just not talked about as much.

Your mom is thinking the same things as your fiancé's mom: is she good enough for him, will she like us, should I ask if I can help? To help ease the tension and break the ice, involve your folks as much as they want to be involved and where they can be involved. If nothing else, keep them informed as to what's happening and where. You might suggest to your bride to ask her mom for her opinion on an item. If you ask simple questions and for opinion only, you can take the advice or leave it. But the point is, you've asked, and that's what matters.

Teddy's Tips

Parents feel left out when there's no communication taking place. Sometimes this can't be helped—perhaps because your parents live out of town—but most times, keeping those lines of communication open can save everyone lots of heartache. And be sure to tell your mom and dad you love them! That always helps.

Who's in Control Here?

One point of battle that might creep into your plans is the "Who's in charge?" theme. You see this wedding as *your* wedding, and rightly so—it should be. You know what you want and don't want for this day. You've taken every precaution to check out references with vendors. You've read articles, been to bridal shows, and interviewed many vendors. You know exactly what you want this day to include, right down to the favors on the table.

The only problem is that your mother might not have read the part that says you're in charge. Your mother may want to be in charge, too. Your mother might hold the checkbook, and the checkbook might have strings attached. It's her one last chance to show her stuff. Your mother may be having a tough time giving up her dominant role. She has taken care of you for all these years and made decisions with your best interests at heart. How could you not want her to make all the arrangements for your wedding, whether you like them or not? Control, power, whatever you want to call it—that's what this is all about. She's afraid of losing her power.

If this sounds like what you're going through, or what you think might happen, try talking with your mother. Sit down with her in a quiet setting; talk calmly and rationally about the wedding plans you've been making. In your most adult, mature voice, let her know (very delicately) that this is your wedding, and while you want her help, it needs to be for items you as a couple want included. (You'll find more practical tips later in this chapter.)

Teddy's Tips

In planning the details of your wedding, patience is indeed a true virtue. Compromise, and don't sweat the small stuff.

Tension Among Parents

Something else I have come to recognize (often on sight) is tension caused by two sets of parents vying for the couple's allegiance. You're no longer dealing with just your parents. All of a sudden, you've got another set of parents to worry about (and possibly stepparents thrown into the mix, which I'll discuss in Chapter 16). The groom might want his parents' names on the invitation because they're paying for the liquor at the reception. The bride's mother, however, might refuse, saying that tradition dictates that only the bride's parents' names appear on the invitation.

Well, dear reader, your parents are (subconsciously) battling out their fear of losing your loyalty. How many times have you heard married friends say, "Oh, our parents are driving us nuts. They both want us to spend Christmas with them. How can we choose?" Well, you have to make a stand, and the sooner the better. It's nothing more than a power struggle over you, the new couple. Your parents are arguing over who will have more control over you after the wedding. They want to be sure you still have allegiance to them.

Just remember that your parents aren't creating all this turmoil intentionally. Often, they don't understand why they behave like they do. Once you understand what's really going on, you can learn to work around it or work with it.

Wedding Woes

As a couple, your primary allegiance needs to be to each other, and you need to present a united front. Avoid problems down the road by deciding early on what limits you will set as a couple regarding the expectations of your respective parents. Try to work things out with parents before you tie the knot, such as alternating holiday visits every other year.

Practical Tips to Get Through It

The closer your wedding day gets, the thicker the tension can become. Here are some practical ideas that might help:

Work on your attitude. Don't think of this wedding as solely *your* day—think of it more as a family affair. It's still your wedding, don't get me wrong, but if you can focus your attention away from yourself, you might be more open to others' suggestions and be willing to compromise.

Remember, above all else, it's the marriage, not the wedding, that's really important. Which gowns are worn, flowers are carried, and entrées are eaten doesn't matter in the end. What matters is the marriage between two people who care, trust, love, and like each other enough to spend the rest of their earthly lives together. That's Commitment, folks, with a capital C.

Put all your cards on the table. Know what you're dealing with and whom. As a united front, you as a couple should approach your families with your wedding desires. See what they're willing to contribute, and take it from there. At least you'll know where you stand. Trying to second-guess your parents is time-consuming and not at all practical. Many couples would rather know what amount of money they have to work with than to guess at what they think they might be working with. You need to know what's what.

Decide which items about the wedding you must have control over and which items you could turn over to your mother or other family members. Don't let your mother feel left out. You want to prevent your mother from feeling insecure, if possible. Insecurity sometimes leads to irrational behavior, and you sure don't need that now. The same advice goes for your partner's mother. One of the fastest ways to make an enemy of your future mother-in-law is to keep her guessing about the wedding plans. Unless she's helping financially, she doesn't have a real decision-making role, but asking her opinion, her advice, and which colors she likes best will help make your relationship stronger and make her feel more a part of the process.

If you and your mother have a huge argument and you hang up the phone or slam the door on her, take a deep breath, count to 100, and call back or walk back in the room. It might be very hard to do, but it will help you in the long haul. Explain that it's the wedding stress that has you bummed out, not her.

Teddy's Tips

Take care of yourself! Stress depletes the body's reserves, so try to get enough rest and exercise and eat properly during the wedding planning. If you aren't physically able to handle all the ups and downs, you'll be more stressed. You can't possibly keep up with the physical drain of wedding planning, plus all the raging emotions, if you're exhausted.

Send your mother a card or flowers, and tell her you love her. Feeling appreciated and loved and knowing that you still care about her goes a long way toward mending fences.

Above all, try to stay calm and be patient with each other. This is normally a stressful time, just given the nature of all that goes on. Don't let a disagreement ruin the fun and excitement of planning for one of the most important days of your life. If you argue, take a deep breath and count to 10 or 100—or even to 1,000, if necessary—and start over. Keep the lines of communication open, and always be willing to listen. Good luck!

Taking some time with their pet, this couple steals away for some time alone.
(PHOTO BY NORTHERN LIGHTS PHOTOGRAPHY)

THE LEAST YOU NEED TO KNOW

- Marriage is one of the basic rites of passage. You're leaving a familiar role and assuming a new role, and it's normal to experience uncertainty and tension on this journey.

- Try to take into consideration the emotions your parents may be experiencing. They don't understand, at least consciously, why they're acting as they are.

- Just understanding that arguments naturally happen during this planning process (and that those arguments are normal) might make this time easier to get through.

- Keep the lines of communication open among both sets of parents, and be sure to tell them how much you love and appreciate them.

- Remember that in the end, it's the marriage that counts, not the wedding. Don't get so caught up in planning the details of the wedding that you forget about the marriage!

CHAPTER 16

I Think I'm Losing My Mind!

In This Chapter

- Understanding and controlling wedding stress
- Dealing with divorced parents and blended families
- Getting help if you need it—and helping yourself
- Deciding on a prenup

*S*tress—it's an everyday word in our society. There is good stress; there is bad stress. And no matter how hard and how well you plan, there is stress during your wedding-planning months.

In this chapter, I talk about what's "normal" wedding stress. We look at divorced and blended families (they're out there everywhere), and I give you some sage advice on how to deal with the stress caused by planning for the happiest day of your life.

Is This Normal?

"I'm stressed to the limit. I just can't take any more!" During the wedding-planning stages, you may find yourself saying this more times than you can count. You may be saying it to family members, to friends, to yourself, and even to perfect strangers.

By their very nature, weddings are stress-producing events. Your emotions are escalated because of the added burdens and worries associated with wedding planning—and that means more stress. Much of the stress comes from all the details you have to be involved with, along with a sense of not having control over all that's going on. You might feel pulled in many directions as well; you have too many advice-givers and not enough supporters. At times, you might even wish that you and your partner had just chosen to elope.

Relax—all these feelings and emotions are in the normal range of wedding stress.

Not every couple experiences prewedding stress. However, if you're like the majority of harried brides in the months before the wedding, you're likely to feel some added anxiety. Let's look at some of the reasons for this stress.

One way of relieving stress during prewedding times is to keep up with your fitness routine.

(PHOTO BY TONY CAMPBELL)

Take some time with your fiancé to do some non-wedding-related activities.

(PHOTO BY TONY CAMPBELL)

It Costs *How Much?*

Think back to Chapter 2, when I talked about the budget and helped you determine what's important to you as a couple and how much you have to spend. Remember when I suggested that you try to stick to that budget?

Going over your budget is one of the biggest stress factors in wedding planning. It's like extending the limit on your credit cards. Then there are all the little extras: garter, guest book, welcome packages at the hotel, parking fees—the list goes on and on. Not expecting the add-on costs and not getting an accurate estimate for a service can leave you drained financially as well as emotionally. This is why keeping your expectations reasonable and setting realistic goals is so important. (Turn to the "Wedding Budget Worksheet" in Appendix A for help figuring out a budget.)

Too Much Advice from Too Many People

When you become engaged, it's like you're suddenly wearing a sign that says, "Advice Needed Here!" You're deluged with all kinds of advice from all kinds of people. In Chapter 1, I suggested that you seek advice from those who had recently married. This is always a good idea, but be prepared for a lot more than you bargained for from other advice-givers.

If you start getting more advice than you need and you start to wonder about your planning, get a grip! Do a reality check!

Relax! Take a deep breath. Let the advice addict's message go in one ear and out the other. Use what you can, and discard the rest. And remember: this, too, shall pass.

Wedding Woes

Don't get bogged down with too much advice from the advice addicts. They might have your best interests at heart, but if you've done your homework, you should be fine.

Trying to Please Everyone

You can't please everyone—and by "everyone" I mean both sets of parents, grandparents, aunts, uncles, cousins, second cousins, second cousins two times removed, all your friends, and your boss—so don't even try.

This is your wedding. Don't lose sight of that now. If you've done your homework, then just go with the flow. Worry about what you as a couple feel is necessary and what you want to include. Do take into consideration your family and their desires or wishes, but the bottom line here is that this is still your wedding. You will drive yourself nuts if you try to meet the demands of the entire family.

How about a picnic in the park? Just the calm water and beautiful surroundings should help soothe prewedding tension.

(PHOTO BY TONY CAMPBELL)

If you run into resistance from family members, be calm, be tactful, be diplomatic, and be firm. Talk it out. But don't alter your plans just to please someone else unless you can make the change without compromising your basic desires.

Divorced and Blended Families

Divorce occurs frequently in this country. If your parents are divorced and have remarried, you have a stepparent and probably some stepbrothers or stepsisters and extended aunts and uncles and grandparents. This is what we, in the wedding industry, refer to as a *blended family*—you know, "yours, mine, and (sometimes) ours."

The sheer numbers added to your family tree can provide plenty of additional stress. But just because parents are divorced it does not mean trouble, come wedding day.

> ## Nuptial Notes
>
> A **blended family** as I refer to it in this book is one in which the parents are divorced and have remarried. Most likely, the individuals bring their own children into the union, so you end up with stepbrothers and stepsisters, as well as grandparents, aunts, uncles, cousins … the whole 9 yards!

When Divorced Parents Get Along

Perhaps your parents have been divorced for many years and are on good speaking terms with each other and you. Both have remarried, and you feel comfortable with your stepparents. When you announce your engagement and sit down to discuss plans, be sure to include both sets of parents—that is, both sets of your parents and your partner's parents. If physical distance separates all of you, be sure you keep both parties informed as to what you discuss and decide, and ask for opinions from all sides. Never put the two sides at odds with each other. Don't compare them with each other.

So many times, having more open communication between the parents is all that's needed. You must be very sure that all your communication between your divorced parents is accurate and complete. Don't expect them to assume anything.

As for finances with divorced parents, let me offer this tip: open a checking account to be used solely for wedding expenses. Have each contributor (your mother, your father, and so on) contribute equal amounts of money to the account. As the wedding bills are paid, each party contributes additional equal amounts to cover other costs. Any money left over might be given to the couple for a nest egg. This helps greatly in alleviating the "But I paid for this!" syndrome.

It's also helpful to chart out who is going to be responsible for each aspect of the wedding expenses. On a piece of paper, make several columns. One column is for the item and the others are for each set of contributors (you, your father, your mother, and so on). Then, go through the list and decide who will be responsible for what. Now you've got it in black and white. Give each contributor a copy of the plan.

When Divorced Parents Don't Get Along

If your divorced parents want nothing to do with one another, accept that fact and work around it. For seating purposes, your mother should be seated in the first row and your father in the second. I have had brides request that their divorced parents be seated together in the first row. It's truly an unselfish act for divorced parents to put aside their anger and support their child, and it's not too much for a child to ask.

Teddy's Tips

If your parents are divorced and not on friendly terms, never assume they'll put aside their differences long enough for you to walk down the aisle. Always use caution, courtesy, and compassion when you discuss your wedding plans with them and how you see their individual roles.

Each wedding with divorced families has a different set of circumstances that must be addressed. You have to be sensitive, to a point, to the wishes of your divorced parents. Be supportive and try to be understanding. If you're faced with dealing with divorced parents and family members during your wedding, try to accommodate their requests. For example, don't put your mother at the same table with your father and his 22-year-old new wife. Even if they get along great, the fact that your new stepmother is younger than the bride might wear a bit on your mom. Use some common sense when dealing with divorced parents. They're still your parents. Hang in there, keep your chin up, and move forward.

If both parents are so bitter that they cannot be trusted to behave themselves at the wedding, ask a neutral third party for advice—perhaps the bridal consultant (trust me, we've seen it all) or the clergy. Parents who declare, "Well, if she's coming then I won't!" may come around if you answer, "I'm sorry to hear that; we'll miss you." This day is about the two of you, not about parents who can't get along. And there's always the chance that despite your worst fears, everyone will get along famously.

Teddy's Tips

For additional help in dealing with divorced family members, check out Cindy Moore's *Planning a Wedding with Divorced Parents* (Three Rivers Press, 1992).

Where to Get Help

All right, I'll admit it. Sometimes these delicate issues can cause hairy situations. What do you do if you need some objective help and guidance? Several options are open to you:

- One of the best places to gather some strength and advice is from your minister, priest, or rabbi.

- Many bridal consultants feel that through our experiences, we should at least have earned our

Ph.D. in human behavior. I've learned many things about human beings and what we can do if pushed hard enough.

- If you aren't comfortable discussing your problems relating to your divorced parents with an officiant or bridal consultant, seek out a trusted family member or a good friend.

Wedding Woes

If you choose to confide in a family member, be certain you can trust that person to be discreet and not share what you've confided.

What You Can Do to Help Yourself

Even if you don't feel the need to talk with a neutral third party, there are several things you and your future spouse can do to help yourselves during this stressful time:

- Get enough sleep and eat right (lots of fruits, veggies, water, and protein-rich foods).

- Get moving—an aerobics class, a walk in the park, swimming, a bike ride in the country … anything to help work off that stress.

- Have fun doing some non-wedding-related things with each other. Take in a movie or sporting event. Get together with friends for a picnic or a night on the town. The only rule: no wedding talk!

- Work on communication skills both with each other and with your parents. Keep those lines of communication open.

- Learn to compromise—give and take.

- Don't lose sight of what is really important—your marriage.

Prenuptial Agreements

In today's society, we're faced daily with very difficult decisions. The prenuptial agreement is a reality, and more couples are being faced with this decision before they marry. This can add more stress than either of you thought possible. This is especially true when a family business is involved whose wealth has reached a point where a future divorce between the couple could be disastrous for the rest of the family.

I know it's hard to think about this at a time when you're madly in love and think that nothing will ever part you, but sometimes, signing off on a prenuptial agreement is the only way you can say, "I do." You might want to check out the books *Don't Get Married Until You Read This* and *Premarital Agreements: When, Why, and How to Write Them.*

Give your sweetie some special time. This bride has just picked a bouquet of wild flowers and shares it with her groom.

(PHOTO BY TONY CAMPBELL)

THE LEAST YOU NEED TO KNOW

- Don't be surprised if you feel overwhelmed and stressed during the planning stages of your wedding. These are normal reactions to this often hectic and emotion-filled time.

- Keep in mind that lots of folks out there are just waiting to give you some advice, whether or not you ask for it. Take what you can use, and let go of the rest.

- When working with divorced family members, be considerate of their feelings. Never compare the parents with each other.

- If your parents are divorced, it's especially important to try to work out potential financial problems before they happen.

- If you're faced with signing a prenuptial agreement, be sure you understand exactly what you're signing and why.

- If you're feeling overwhelmed by stress, talking to an objective listener can help.

CHAPTER 17

Much Ado About Everything:
Prenuptial Preparation

IN THIS CHAPTER

- Practicing at the wedding rehearsal
- Getting yourself ready for the big day
- Reducing your stress level
- Making it down the aisle in time

I've discussed nearly all the details you need to know to help you prepare for your wedding. Now, you're zeroing in on the big day. Preparation is the name of the game; it has been all along. Now, even more than ever, I want you to prepare just a little bit more as you move right up to the big day!

This chapter focuses on getting yourself ready for your wedding day, reducing your stress level, and getting down the aisle on time (it's not as easy as it sounds). I talk about how important the rehearsal is and what you need to do after all the prewedding festivities.

This beautiful bride is putting on the final touches.

(PHOTO BY FOTOBRICENO)

The Rehearsal

The wedding rehearsal is an important event in the wedding-planning process. It's your insurance policy that the members of your wedding cast know their lines, places, cues, what to do, and what *not* to do come wedding day.

The wedding rehearsal usually but not always occurs the day or evening before the wedding is to take place. Many times, the Jewish rehearsal takes place the morning of the wedding. Plan the rehearsal for whatever time your individual circumstances dictate.

Practice Makes Perfect

The whole purpose of the wedding rehearsal is to practice what will take place during the ceremony. As in a play rehearsal, the director (officiant or bridal consultant) conducts the rehearsal so all the characters (wedding party) know their parts, responsibilities, and duties.

Her pearls and hair stickpins lie on the leather and lace gloves she will wear.

(PHOTO BY FOTOBRICENO)

It helps if the musicians are present for the rehearsal. One of the prime functions of the rehearsal is to practice both the processional (when the wedding party enters) and the recessional (when the wedding party exits).

Who Should Attend?

Those who should attend the wedding rehearsal include the following:

- All members of the wedding party, including ushers, the flower girl, and the ring bearer
- Readers
- The soloist
- Musicians
- The officiant
- Your parents

Who's the Boss Here?

Over the years, I've found that the best rehearsals are the ones conducted by the person who will perform the wedding service, usually the officiant. Some facilities have a wedding director on staff who oversees the rehearsal. If that's the case with your ceremony site, work with that person. Also, if you've hired a bridal consultant, be sure she knows her role at the rehearsal.

Whatever circumstances you face, go in with a positive attitude. Try to work out all the ceremony details long before the rehearsal. It does little good for you or the officiant to be deciding on reading selections the eve of your wedding. If at all possible, get those items ironed out beforehand.

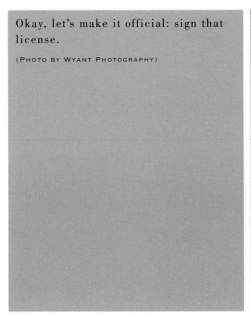

Okay, let's make it official: sign that license.

(PHOTO BY WYANT PHOTOGRAPHY)

Getting Ready

Okay, time is marching on. You've made it through the rehearsal in one piece, and you have been the honored guests at a lovely rehearsal dinner (see Chapter 6). You say good night and head home for some much-needed rest.

I've tried to emphasize throughout this book how important it is for you to be organized. I don't keep repeating that phrase because I have a limited vocabulary. I say this because, of all the ways you can help yourself, staying organized and knowing what to do is the key to a successful, stress-free wedding day.

Teddy's Tips

Use the checklist in Appendix B to help you keep track of all the details in the months leading up to the big event. Keep it handy, and refer to it often!

You Are Getting Sleepy …

When you come home (or back to the hotel—wherever you're staying the night before your wedding), take a nice, relaxing bath. You need to be relaxed so you can get some much-needed sleep.

While you're taking it easy in the tub, try sipping some warm milk (not chocolate, which contains caffeine) or some herbal tea. Put on some soft music to help set the mood, or listen to a relaxation tape. This is "be good to yourself" time. Indulge yourself. Try to block out every possible negative vision you can. You want to be at peace, inside and out.

When you finish with your bath, follow your normal nighttime routine. Get as much sleep as possible. The wedding day will be exciting but exhausting. You need a lot of sleep now so you can feel and look great in the morning. A bride or groom with dark circles under their eyes from lack of sleep is not a pretty sight.

You Are What You Eat

Just as important as enough rest is the right kind of food in your body. As I've mentioned in previous chapters, you must keep yourself on track by eating right and getting enough rest.

Even if you're not a breakfast person, try to be one on your wedding day. Even if it's just a bagel and some juice, get a little something in your tummy. Believe me, depending on the time of your service, there might not be time to eat later, or you might be too nervous.

Teddy's Tips

If your wedding is later in the day, be sure to bring some healthful snacks to the ceremony site for the wedding party to nibble on. Saltines or crackers, nuts, cheese cubes, and fresh fruit are all good choices.

Making a List and Checking It Twice

By now you should have a checklist of what goes to the church with you, what goes to the reception, and what goes on the honeymoon. Just as I keep emphasizing to keep yourself organized, keeping a list and adding items to it as you think of them helps keep your stress level down and gets you to the church on time and with what you need.

Something Old, Something New

Whether you choose to dress at home or at the wedding facility, be sure to include in the bag of tricks you're taking with you the items in the verse "Something old, something new, something borrowed, something blue, and a lucky penny in your shoe."

"Something old" is used to show a sense of continuity. You can use a family heirloom or carry the family Bible or Prayer Book.

"Something new" equates to hope for an optimistic future. Most brides consider their wedding gown their "something new."

"Something borrowed" refers to the superstition that happiness wears off on others. So if you borrow something from someone who is happy or from a happily married friend, you'll have a happy future, too.

For "something blue," brides include a blue item of some kind to bolster the favorite old line, "Those who dress in blue have lovers true." Blue has long been considered the color of fidelity, purity, and love. Many brides choose to wear a blue garter.

In England, "a penny in your shoe" is a sixpence; in Canada, it's a quarter. No matter what the coin, the idea is to ensure a fortuitous married life.

The Emergency Kit

Ah, the emergency kit. If you've hired a bridal consultant to coordinate the weekend activities, you can skip this section; she should take care of having these items available for you.

If you're braving this adventure on your own, take heed. Some items you'll need at the ceremony site, just for insurance. Of course, you won't need all these things, but it's a good idea to have them, just in case:

- Small sewing kit

- Small scissors

- Safety pins of various sizes

- Tissues

- Masking tape and a stapler (You might be surprised at the repairs you can make with these items.)

- Hand towel

- Wash cloth
- Soft drinks/juice/bottled water
- Saltine crackers (to alleviate nausea)
- Static-cling spray
- Breath mints or mouthwash
- Tampons or sanitary supplies (You never know.)

Being prepared, both physically and emotionally, and staying organized are ways to keep you on track for your wedding day. It's time-consuming, but it pays off when you glide down that aisle relatively stress-free and looking wonderful.

Time to Get Dressed!

This is one time in your life when I want you to pamper yourself. This is not the time to be running back and forth setting up the reception décor and then rushing to get ready. This is *your* day, and you owe it to yourself to take your time and savor preparing for your marriage.

Most brides have their hair done professionally at the salon, or the hairdresser comes to the ceremony site or home to prepare the bride. This is a great treat. The same goes for your makeup. Your wedding day makeup should not be dramatically different from what you normally wear. You want to look natural and like you. You will need a little more lipstick color than normal simply because of photos. Having a makeup artist apply the makeup is also a wonderful treat. Again, try out your makeup before the wedding day.

Wedding Woes

Practice walking in your wedding shoes before the ceremony not only to be sure they're comfortable, but also to scuff up the soles a bit. Brand-new soles are smooth and can be slippery; a scuffed sole has more traction and can prevent a fall.

Our bride is getting ready, having her hair done. Notice that she's wearing a top she can easily slip off so she doesn't mess up her hair.

(PHOTO BY EMILY'S IMAGES)

A quiet moment with Dad. He just gave her a bracelet for a wedding gift. Moments like these are meant to be captured on film.

(PHOTO BY EMILY'S IMAGES)

Mom helping her daughter get ready for this all-important day.

(PHOTO BY MELANIE MAUER PHOTOGRAPHY)

So you've got your hair done, veil on, makeup looks great, and you're ready to put on the gown. Be careful not to get makeup on the gown! You'll need help here (that's where your trusted bridesmaids come in handy).

The final touch is jewelry. The pieces you choose to wear with your wedding gown should accent the gown, not detract from it. You might want to wear gloves if the gown is strapless. When you're all ready, go look in the mirror and see the princess gazing back at you!

Taking That Long Walk

You're all dressed and ready to go. You've had all your pictures taken before the ceremony (see Chapter 10). You've spent some quiet time with your bridesmaids getting ready, and now comes the moment you've dreamed about for years. Your bridal consultant or the church's wedding coordinator gets everybody lined up for the processional.

The music starts for the grandmothers, and they are seated. The moms are next to be seated. Maybe they'll light the family candles for the unity candle if you're following that tradition. Next comes the processional for the men and the officiant, followed by your bridesmaids and flower girls and ring bearers. Finally, you hear the swell of the organ, the trumpets sound,

you get chills, and your tummy is doing flip-flops. All of a sudden your dad takes your arm and you are off to meet your groom, the man with whom you will share the rest of your life.

Don't worry about another thing. Once you reach the altar, you will be in the officiant's hands and I'll bet he's never lost a couple at the altar yet. Take his or her direction as you move through the ceremony, and try to savor this time. It will go by so fast, later on it will seem like a blur.

Then it's time for the kiss, and you're married. Congratulations! Now go enjoy the biggest party you'll ever have!

The exchange of rings. Notice the bride is wearing a veil that covers her face.

(PHOTO BY CRAIG PAUL STUDIO)

This is a new trend—a streamer release. Guests are handed little packages of streamers and, on cue, they flip them open and the streamers unfurl, hopefully on the couple.

(PHOTO BY COLTER PHOTOGRAPHY)

THE LEAST YOU NEED TO KNOW

- The rehearsal is a very important part of the wedding activities. Just as an actor wouldn't go onstage without rehearsing his or her lines, don't show up for your wedding day unprepared.

- Be sure everyone who needs to be at the rehearsal is there, including all members of the wedding party and, if possible, the musicians.

- The person officiating at the wedding should be the person in charge of the rehearsal. Work with your officiant to make the rehearsal go as smoothly as possible.

- One of the best ways to help get you ready for your big day is to get enough sleep the night before and eat a good breakfast the morning of the wedding.

- Be sure to put together a kit of emergency items to take along to the ceremony site for last-minute crises.

- Allow plenty of time to dress for your wedding so you don't feel rushed. Pamper yourself!

Extra Special Weddings

IN THIS PART

18 What's in a Theme?

19 Mickey and Minnie, Here We Come:
Destination Weddings

Part 5 talks about all special weddings. I share theme-wedding ideas, including holiday, outdoor, military, and the latest trend—the personalized themed wedding. I talk about what you need to know to pull off a weekend wedding or a destination wedding. Read on and learn!

CHAPTER 18

What's in a Theme?

IN THIS CHAPTER

- Considering a theme wedding
- Getting ideas for seasonal, outdoor, military, and personalized wedding themes
- Planning a theme wedding
- Throwing a weekend wedding

Weddings with themes are big these days. Brides and grooms want to create a unique atmosphere for their big day and are choosing themes around which they can build this atmosphere. Couples often select a wedding theme based on a particular season or date. One of the biggest trends in weddings today is personalizing the wedding around the couple's likes, careers, or family heritage. That can start the wedding theme idea.

In this chapter, I also discuss the increasingly popular weekend wedding and share some ideas for making it a delight for all involved.

Seasonal Weddings

A seasonal wedding is one that takes place near a certain holiday or during a certain season of the year. Examples of holidays around which you might choose to hold your wedding include the following:

- Christmas

- New Year's (both eve and day)

- Valentine's Day

- Fourth of July

- Halloween

In the following sections, I share with you some ideas for planning a wedding around each of these holidays.

Christmas Weddings

Christmas weddings, in particular, can be wonderfully romantic. The season seems especially filled with love, hope, and peace, and those sentiments tend to shine through weddings held during this time. Most facilities and churches decorate for the holiday, which can add a special and lovely touch to your wedding festivities (and save you money on decorations).

This church is decorated very nicely for a Christmas wedding. Notice all the detail on the aisle candles.

(PHOTO FROM THE AUTHOR'S COLLECTION)

A red Christmas tree adds color to this holiday wedding.

(PHOTO BY RANDY BICK PHOTOGRAPHY)

Here are some additional touches to consider for a Christmas wedding:

- Ask musicians to play Christmas carols during the prelude.

- Have a children's choir sing carols among guests at the reception.

- Print Christmas song sheets on parchment paper, tie with red velvet ribbon, and use as favors.

- Tie the programs with plaid Christmas ribbon.

- Use a small wreath tied with tiny bells and ribbons as favors.

- Have ornaments printed with your names and hang them on a tree for guests to take as they leave.

- Dress your bridesmaids in the traditional black velvet with Christmas plaid.

- Tuck small silver bells or other holiday ornaments among the flowers in the bouquets.

- Use different sizes of wrapped packages or miniature decorated Christmas trees for the table centerpieces.

- Decorate with lots of white lights, icicle lights, and candles.

- Carry a white muff instead of a bouquet.

At the reception, this Christmas bride filled hurricane globes with Christmas ornaments and red holly berries. Very simple, but very pretty.

(PHOTO BY RAAB)

New Year's Eve or New Year's Day Weddings

You can create a special atmosphere planning a New Year's wedding, whether on New Year's Eve or New Year's Day. Here are some ideas for New Year's weddings:

- In the center of the dance floor, have a huge sack of balloons tied up, ready to release at the stroke of midnight.

- Have guests make New Year's resolutions at their tables, seal them in envelopes, and leave them in a basket by the door. Later in January, mail the resolutions out to your guests as a reminder of the resolution and of your wedding.

- Decorate with lots of confetti, noisemakers, and balloons.

This photo of a place setting shows more detail, including a small bouquet and the gold ware (silver ware). Not only is it beautiful, but festive, too.

(PHOTO BY RANDY BICK PHOTOGRAPHY)

These tables are decorated for New Year's Eve. Notice all the gold accents, including music notes and gold charger plates. Looks like they'll ring in the new year with a classic touch.

(PHOTO BY RANDY BICK PHOTOGRAPHY)

Party on!

(PHOTO BY RANDY BICK PHOTOGRAPHY)

Valentine's Day Weddings

Valentine's Day is already a romantic holiday; add a wedding to the day, and you have the setting for some special happenings. Here are some ideas to consider for a Valentine's Day wedding:

- Consider a wedding gown in a pale shade of pink or accented with pink.

- Dress your bridesmaids in varying shades of pink or the traditional Valentine's Day red velvet.

- Use heart-shape everything at the wedding and reception: candelabrum, unity candles, guest book, napkins, candy favors … or have two hearts printed on the programs.

Fourth of July Weddings

Talk about fireworks! As the ceremony ends and the officiant pronounces you husband and wife, what's more appropriate than an outdoors fireworks display? Here are some more Fourth of July theme ideas:

- It's July, so why not plan for an outdoor reception with red, white, and blue tablecloths?

- Lead off the processional with a 1776 traditional drum and fife core. Consider using the "1812 Overture" for the recessional. How majestic!

- Have your gown and those of your wedding party made in an eighteenth-century style.

- Top off the wedding cake with sparklers, and give children some sparklers to enjoy, too (with adult supervision).

- Right before you and your new groom make your exit, gather the entire reception out on the lawn and have a fireworks display to bring your wonderful day to a dramatic end.

Wedding Woes

Do *not* try setting off your own fireworks. Leave any fireworks displays to the pros!

What better ending to a Fourth of July wedding than exiting amid fireworks and sparklers?

(PHOTO BY BROADWAY PHOTOGRAPHY)

Halloween Weddings

A Halloween wedding theme might include guests coming in costumes. The waitstaff might be dressed in costume also. Some other traditional Halloween elements you could include are as follows:

- Feature candy apples, wrapped in colorful cellophane and tied with a ribbon, as favors.

- Decorate with a black and orange color scheme or other rich fall colors.

- Use corn stalks and pumpkins nestled together around the room for décor. The occasional scarecrow is fun, too.

- Have an assortment of Halloween masks for guests to use, waiting for them at their tables or at the place card table (if you're using assigned seating). How fun for guests to don masks in the celebration of your marriage!

- Feature baskets of nuts and berries or an overflowing cornucopia as part of the table centerpieces.

- For favors, leave Halloween treat bags filled with goodies at each place setting for your guests with a note from you and your partner.

Not every wedding is white and pastel with pretty flowers and a dreamlike feel. Check out these wedding photos—talk about a theme wedding!

(PHOTOS BY MONIQUE FEIL)

Notice the candleholders here; the sign represents the table name. Now there's a comforting feeling ....

What a clever way to assign places. The guest's first name is at the bottom, with their last name initial at the top.

Outdoor and Garden Weddings

Outdoor and garden weddings are probably the most difficult to plan and riskiest to carry out. For some reason, people seem to feel that if they opt for an outdoor wedding in Grandma's lovely garden, it somehow will be easier and cheaper than renting a facility and a reception hall. Nothing could be further from the truth!

Teddy's Tips

Choosing an outdoor wedding does not mean it will necessarily be cheaper or less elaborate than an indoor wedding. A great deal depends on your geographic location. If you live in a climate such as California, where the weather is not a major risk factor, planning an outdoor wedding is an easier task. If your wedding will be in the Northeast, however, be prepared for a sudden rainstorm, a chilling cold front, or a sticky heat wave.

This wedding used a Hawaiian theme. The bride, groom and flower girl all have matching Hawaiian clothes.

(PHOTO BY THE WEDDING CASA)

These little umbrellas are actually the table assignment cards. Cute idea!

(PHOTO BY THE WEDDING CASA)

Unpredictable Mother Nature

The first thing to consider when scheduling an outdoor wedding is a backup plan for the ceremony and the reception. Do you have a tent in place or a church reserved in case of bad weather? This is an important agenda item. You just can't depend on Mother Nature to cooperate!

Dealing with outdoor weddings can be made a little easier if you have the budget. Tents can be floored so the water level won't cause your guests any discomfort. (Flooring for tents is very expensive, though.) Tents can also be heated or cooled.

Bouquet Toss

Superstition says that if it *does* rain on your wedding day, it's a sign of good fortune. That's putting a positive spin on it!

What You'll Need

Also with outdoor weddings is the need to bring everything outside; you must be completely self-sufficient. Here's a partial list of what you'll need:

- Portable toilets
- Lighting
- Tables and chairs
- Linens
- Décor
- Food and beverages
- Kitchen tent (for preparing the food)

You also want to be sure you have the bug population under control in the area. Have a professional come to the site several weeks before the event to determine what you need to have controlled. Always let the professionals deal with insecticides.

Teddy's Tips

Decide on one focal point for the actual service so your guests can focus their attention on the wedding party. Try for something natural: a grouping of trees, a fountain, or the head of a garden. You're outside, so you don't want to compete with Mother Nature—just enhance her.

Park It Here, My Dear

Depending on your property and the size of your guest list, parking can be a major problem. Wherever you schedule the outdoor wedding, make doubly sure you have adequate parking facilities and attendants.

If the logistics can be worked out, consider having valet parking. This is a great idea, especially if you have a tight area to put lots of cars. Be sure to check with your insurance carrier about the liability of hiring valet parkers.

Another solution is to run a shuttle from a local parking lot (for example, a school or a church) to the site. (Check with local authorities in case you need a special permit.) Then hire a company to operate a van or bus.

Tears Over Melting Tiers

When choosing your menu for your outdoor wedding, keep in mind that it's going to be outside. You know, among nature—the birds, the bees, the bugs. And the heat. Hire a reputable caterer to recommend a menu that will hold up under the warm-weather sun.

Getting Personal

Personalizing your wedding is another way to "theme" the wedding. You can develop any type of wedding theme as much as you want. You might use only a hint of a theme, or you might go all out and make it a truly thematic wedding from start to finish. The choice is yours.

Teddy's Tips

When you've chosen a theme for your wedding, search the Internet for information and ideas (see Chapter 1).

The Weekend Wedding

A weekend wedding offers your guests additional activities throughout the weekend beyond the normal wedding festivities. This type of wedding is becoming more and more popular as families come from all over the country to attend a wedding. Instead of attending only the wedding and the reception, your wedding guests can choose to participate in several preplanned functions. The wedding and reception are the highlights of the activities, but you can plan other outings to help guests put aside their hectic schedules for a little while and provide them with a mini-vacation.

Guest Activities

Your guest activities for a weekend wedding can be as unique as the two of you and the location you've chosen. You can arrange those activities around a theme or a time of the year.

You don't have to have your weekend wedding in a big city around something like Notre Dame. You can do exactly the same type of weekend wedding using what you have in your area.

This groom owns a dry cleaner. And that's where this couple was married.

(PHOTO BY MONIQUE FEIL)

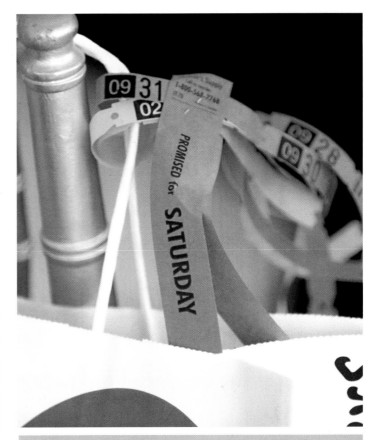

Even the pick-up tag says, "Promised for Saturday"—very clever.

(PHOTO BY MONIQUE FEIL)

Meanwhile, back in the tent, guests will receive their gift bag, which says, "We love our customers (friends)."

(PHOTO BY MONIQUE FEIL)

Here are some other ideas you could incorporate into your weekend wedding activities:

- Set up a softball game—maybe a tournament.
- Take a trip to the local zoo.
- Tour a historical district.
- Spend a day at a spa and treat your wedding party to the works: a manicure, pedicure, and body massage.
- Have a picnic or barbecue in a park or backyard.
- Go see a play.
- Have a scavenger hunt through the city with prizes.

Teddy's Tips

Be sure to check with the local chamber of commerce for other events scheduled for the same weekend as your wedding. If you can stay away from busy times in your chosen city, you'll be better off.

Hear Ye! Hear Ye!

When planning for the weekend wedding (whether you're having it in your home city with family and friends coming in from all over, or you've made arrangements for it in another location), you should follow some do's and don'ts. Always think of your guests' comfort and enjoyment during the weekend, and be sure to take care of their needs.

Here are some additional things to help make everyone's visit more pleasurable:

Get a good travel agent to coordinate the hotel, airlines, shuttle service, and car rentals.

Get the word out early by using a save-the-date card.

Send a newsletter a month before the wedding, including details about parties and other events, weather conditions, hotel information, and maps.

Make guests feel welcome when they arrive. Place some kind of welcome package in their hotel rooms. (See Chapter 12 for ideas on creating a welcome basket.)

Leave copies of the wedding weekend agenda at the hotel's front desk, in the hospitality room, and with both sets of parents.

Provide a list of baby-sitters, or make sitter arrangements for those guests who are bringing small children for the weekend.

Have some of the activities geared toward children. Consider hiring a social director to come in and organize a children's party for the kids while the adults are entertained somewhere else.

Try not to overplan. You want to offer activities to your guests so they can take part, but they shouldn't feel overwhelmed.

Remember that the wedding and the reception are the high points of the weekend. Everything else is optional for most of your guests.

Weekend weddings are meant to encompass all the beauty, love, and grace a one-day wedding holds, plus give your guests more of a feel for celebrating in a variety of ways. Do your homework, stay organized, and plan ahead. You can then relax and enjoy what should be a memorable weekend for everyone involved!

THE LEAST YOU NEED TO KNOW

- Build your theme wedding around you and your partner's heritage, hobby, or career. Make it unique to the two of you.

- Seasonal weddings are a natural idea if you want to give your wedding a theme. You can have some fun picking a date to plan your wedding around and decorating with seasonal motifs.

- Outdoor weddings can be beautiful and fun, but they are risky. Always have a backup plan in case the weather doesn't cooperate.

- Remember that the wedding and the reception are the highlights of the wedding weekend. No other activity should overshadow these two events.

- Don't overplan your weekend wedding. Maintain a balance in your agenda. Consider your guests' interests and needs; give them time to rest and relax.

CHAPTER 19

Mickey and Minnie, Here We Come:
Destination Weddings

IN THIS CHAPTER

- Planning a destination wedding
- Arranging activities for your guests
- Doing some research
- Looking at some popular destinations

I talked about weekend weddings in Chapter 18. A destination wedding is very similar to a weekend wedding in format and principle; the primary difference between the two is the kind of location you choose for the wedding.

Like a weekend wedding, a destination wedding should offer fun and relaxation for everyone involved. These weddings also require some extra time and organization to pull off successfully. In this chapter, I tell you all you need to know!

What Is a Destination Wedding?

A *destination wedding* takes place somewhere where you might take a vacation. A vacation in Eugene, Oregon, or Portland, Maine, might not be at the top of your list, but you definitely would consider a vacation to Disney World in Florida or the Hawaiian islands. Think of it this way: with a destination wedding, the majority of activities you can offer your guests are already in place.

For example, let's say you're a big country music fan. What better spot could you find than Nashville, Tennessee, and Opryland to enhance your destination wedding dreams? Nashville is a stately southern city filled with beautiful plantations, and it's the center of the country music industry. Think of all the activities right at your fingertips!

A destination wedding can be as elaborate or as simple as you want, depending on your budget. Many times, families take extended vacations at resort spots and include the wedding festivities.

Keep in mind that with destination weddings, your guests are responsible for their own transportation costs and housing expenses.

Nuptial Notes

A **destination wedding** sometimes is referred to as a travel wedding (because you travel to the location) or a honeymoon wedding (because the destination also serves as your honeymoon spot).

Here's a dad and a groom right before the ceremony. Notice that Dad is dressed casually—island attire, you know.

(PHOTO BY WILLIS)

Tips on Planning a Destination Wedding

There are several items to think about when planning a destination wedding. The following sections contain some key considerations.

Do Your Research!

If you have an area in mind or have some interest you want to fulfill, start arranging for your destination wedding by doing research:

- Check out websites.
- Talk with other couples who have gone to the same area or resort.
- Contact the tourism boards.
- Contact the local chamber of commerce.
- Check on marriage requirements.
- If you are a member of AAA (American Automobile Association) or another travel club, check with them for ideas and details. Most times their advice and information is free to members. They can also send you travel guides and maps of the area or resort.

Mother Nature ... Again

Think about the weather conditions where you're hoping to hold your wedding. Maybe a wedding planned for a remote beach in hurricane season isn't such a good idea. A veil blowing gently in the breeze is one thing, but gale-force winds could be overkill. Get some expert advice about the weather at the location you're thinking of at the time of year you're considering.

Here comes the bride ...

(PHOTO BY WILLIS)

A Place in Your Heart

When choosing a location, think about a spot that might have some meaning to you. If "Cinderella" was your favorite fairy tale when you were a little girl, you might choose a place like Disney World.

Or if your family always took skiing vacations, you might consider a place like Aspen, Colorado, for your destination wedding. Consider what's meaningful to the two of you.

Ah, the princess arrives. Cinderella's dreams come true at Walt Disney World. This bride and groom arrive in the famous coach pulled by six white horses.

(PHOTO FROM THE AUTHOR'S COLLECTION)

Accommodations and Amenities

After you choose a location, you need to select the accommodations you'll use. If you have more specific choices to make, such as choosing a particular Hawaiian or Caribbean island, then you'll want to do more research to find just the right resort for your wedding.

Wedding Woes

When selecting the hotel or resort for your destination wedding, be sure you read and fully understand the fine print in the contracts. Trust me, there's a reason it's so small!

Is It Legal?

Just because you have every detail in place and have talked at length with the hotel and the airlines, don't make that first deposit until you're sure you can be married in your chosen spot. Find out the rules and regulations of marrying at the site you've chosen. Rules vary from state to state and from island to island. Take some time now to determine whether your dream location actually can become a reality.

Guest Activities

Unlike the agenda for a weekend wedding, your guest activities are readily available with a destination wedding. Because of the locale you've chosen, planning activities to keep you and your guests busy will not be a chore.

Let the destination determine what activities you'll have guests involved with. The choices are endless. It's up to you and your groom and just takes a little imagination.

What a photograph! Beautiful blue water, blue sky, gentle breeze, and "I do."

(PHOTO BY WILLIS)

Practical Tips

To make your dreams come true of having your wedding and reception on an island paradise or with a castle as a backdrop, you'll need to be sure you have all your bases covered. Here are some suggestions to help you utilize your resources and still get to the church on time:

Work with the local chamber of commerce or tourist board.

Hire a bridal consultant from that locale. Many times, hotels can provide names of local consultants. You can also obtain names of bridal consultants in a particular locale or who specialize in destination weddings by contacting the Association of Bridal Consultants at 860-355-0464 or BridalAssn@aol.com.

Whether you choose to work with a private company or a staff member at the resort, be sure you write down all your questions before you contact the bridal consultant. Include all the items you need to discuss: ceremony site, music, floral arrangements, photography, videography, food, liquor, and the fee for staff. You don't want any surprises 2,000 miles away from home. Get those details in writing now.

Be sure you have the legal requirements for marrying in that locale in writing. Work out all these kinks ahead of time!

If at all possible, make a trip to the site before the wedding just to be sure everything is as you want it and there are no hidden agendas with hotel staff.

Be sure to send a newsletter to those guests who have indicated they would like to share in your destination wedding. In the newsletter, include information on airlines, hotels, costs, choices of accommodations, what's available onsite, dress style for the stay, and anything pertaining specifically to that destination. You can enclose a brochure of the hotel or resort in the newsletter to entice those guests even more.

Be sure your arrangements are confirmed and you have everything in writing. Look over contracts very carefully. Read the fine print—you don't want any surprises.

If you're bringing your wedding gown with you, put it in a garment bag and hang it on the plane. Linens and silk taffeta are not good fabric choices for travel; stick with cotton, satin, cotton voile, or a silk crepe for the least amount of upkeep. Check with the hotel or resort about pressing or steaming services.

Popular Sites

You can consider any resort area that can accommodate a wedding for your destination wedding. Choose the wedding site as you would choose your honeymoon site. What activities are you interested in? What activities would you like for your guests? Is there a fantasy you would like to fulfill, such as spending time exploring a

The exchanging of the vows. They look pretty serious.
(PHOTO BY WILLIS)

castle, snorkeling off the coast of St. Thomas, or deep-sea fishing in the waters of Bermuda? Whatever your fantasy is, see if you can find someplace that fulfills it.

This doesn't have to be a big-time resort, either. If you find a state park or nature area particularly inviting and you can envision yourself surrounded by family and friends on top of a mountain, go for it. Make this your special time, and offer your guests the opportunity to participate with you as you celebrate your wedding.

Some popular destination wedding sites include the following:

- Disney World
- The Sandals Resorts
- Disney Land
- Las Vegas
- Hawaii
- Cruise ship

And speaking of cruise ships, the romantic notion of being married by the cruise ship's captain is false.

Teddy's Tips

A fascinating book by Hannelore Hahn, *Places*, now in its eighth edition, might help you find a unique destination for your wedding. The book's subtitle says it all: "A Directory of Public Places for Private Events and Private Places for Public Functions."

Unless he is a notary public or an ordained minister, the captain cannot perform the service. Most couples have the ceremony dockside—off the ship—and then go aboard and have the reception, followed by days at sea for the honeymoon.

A destination wedding can be fun, romantic, and intimate for all involved. It can be a wonderful vacation idea for guests and a good opportunity for family and friends to get to know one another. Your

Quiet—ceremony taking place.

(PHOTO BY WILLIS)

This evergreen inside the Grand Floridian has been sculpted to resemble Cinderella's Castle.

(PHOTO FROM THE AUTHOR'S COLLECTION)

options are endless and can be as exotic or out of the ordinary as your budget allows. Whatever destination you choose, just be sure to do your homework—and enjoy!

Some Final Thoughts

Over the past 22 years, I've learned so much about people, about commitment, and about what is really important to a wedding, the celebration that follows, and life in general. I've worked with some of the most absolutely delightful couples in the world. The trust and respect they have given to me makes me very humble. No amount of money could ever give me the satisfaction I've received from working with these fine young men and women and being honored by them to help with one of the most important days in their lives.

The weddings you just read about are all different and unique to the particular couple—and they should be. This is your wedding—make it part of the two of you. It still amazes me how very different we all are and how we can take that uniqueness and use it to make the magical essence of our own weddings.

Enjoy this planning time. Spend it wisely, and savor this experience with each other. And I do sincerely hope that all your dreams come true and you live happily ever after. With blessings and my very best wishes!

THE LEAST YOU NEED TO KNOW

- Destination weddings offer a vacation atmosphere and many of the activities you might want to schedule for your guests.

- Be sure you check about legal requirements for the marriage license in the locale in which you plan to have your wedding.

- Wherever you decide to have your destination wedding, work with a bridal consultant either from that area or someone who specializes in destination weddings. The bridal consultant can be invaluable in helping you achieve the type of wedding you desire.

- Try to visit the site before the wedding to be sure it's what you have in mind, and to be sure you have accurately communicated your desires to the local staff.

- Allow enough time for your guests to plan for a destination wedding; send them informative newsletters to help them prepare months in advance.

Wedding
Worksheets

Throughout the book, I talk about keeping yourself organized all through the process leading up to your big day. The worksheets in this appendix help you with that organization. Each worksheet refers to the chapter where that specific material is discussed. For example, catering is discussed in Chapter 7, so if you have questions as you're filling in the catering worksheet, you can turn back to Chapter 7 for help. And although it's not technically a worksheet, at the end of this appendix, I included a handy list that tells who pays for what.

These worksheets are meant to be used. They're not here to add pages or just to look pretty. Using them will help you so much in the long run as you choose and work with different vendors. Good luck!

Bridal Consultant Worksheet (Chapter 1)

Name of consultant: _____

Telephone: _____ Cell: _____ Fax: _____

Address: _____

Website: _____ E-mail: _____

Referred by: _____ Number of years in business: _____

Number of weddings coordinated: _____ Does he/she belong to a professional organization? _____

What plans or packages does he/she offer? _____

Fees: _____ Contract signed and returned with retainer (date): _____

Notes: _____

_____

_____

_____

_____

_____

Catering Worksheet (Chapter 7)

Name of caterer: _____

Address: _____

Telephone: _____ Fax: _____ E-mail: _____

Menu format: Buffet _____   Hors d'oeuvres _____   Served dinner _____   Other: _____

Menu ideas: _____

_____

_____

Cost per person: _____ Deposit made: _____ Balance due: _____

Guarantee of numbers due: _____ Next appointment with chef: _____

Notes: _____

_____

_____

_____

_____

_____

_____

_____

_____

_____

_____

Ceremony Site Worksheet (Chapter 3)

Name of facility: _____

Address: _____

Telephone: _____ Fax: _____ E-mail: _____

Contact: _____

Meeting(s) with contact: _____ Date(s) available: _____

Fee: _____

Includes:

Organist ____   Officiant ____   Custodian ____   Kneeler ____   Aisle cloths ____   Candelabra ____

Other: _____

Number of guests facility can accommodate: _____

Musical equipment provided: _____

Dressing room facilities: _____

Parking areas: _____

Wedding policy booklets: _____

Facility restrictions: _____

_____

Added fees for rental items (candelabra, kneeler, aisle cloth, etc.): _____

_____

Special accommodations for people with disabilities (parking, access, restrooms, etc.): _____

_____

_____

Notes: _____

_____

_____

_____

_____

_____

_____

_____

_____

_____

_____

_____

_____

_____

_____

_____

_____

Choosing the Reception Site Worksheet (Chapter 4)

Facility: _____

Contact: _____

Telephone: _____ Fax: _____ E-mail: _____

Rental price: _____

Includes:

      Linens ____   Tables ____   Security ____

      Skirting ____   Chairs ____   Plants, decorative items ____

Ample parking? _____ Distance from ceremony: _____

Catering requirements: _____

      In-house: _____

      Outside: _____

Number of restrooms: _____ Accessible to people with disabilities? _____

Date available: _____

Notes: _____

_____

_____

_____

_____

_____

Cost Comparison Worksheet (Chapter 2)

Item	Vendor Name and Contact	Cost Estimate
Jewelry store:		
Engagement ring	_____	_____
Wedding rings	_____	_____
Bridal consultant	_____	_____
	_____	_____
Ceremony site rental	_____	_____
	_____	_____
Reception site	_____	_____
	_____	_____
Caterer	_____	_____
	_____	_____
Bridal shop:		
Gown	_____	_____
Veil	_____	_____
Attendants' dresses	_____	_____

Item	Vendor Name and Contact	Cost Estimate
Wedding stationery:		
Invitations	_____	_____
Announcements	_____	_____
Enclosures	_____	_____
Other paper	_____	_____
Photographer	_____	_____
	_____	_____
Videographer	_____	_____
	_____	_____
Florist	_____	_____
	_____	_____
	_____	_____
Musicians:		
Ceremony	_____	_____
	_____	_____
Reception	_____	_____
	_____	_____
Wedding cake	_____	_____
	_____	_____
Groom's cake	_____	_____
	_____	_____
Attendants' gifts	_____	_____
	_____	_____
Men's formal wear	_____	_____
	_____	_____
Party rental equipment	_____	_____
	_____	_____
Limousine	_____	_____
	_____	_____
Favors	_____	_____
	_____	_____
Programs	_____	_____
	_____	_____
Honeymoon:		
Hotel	_____	_____
Travel	_____	_____
Tours	_____	_____
Wardrobe	_____	_____

Item	Vendor Name and Contact	Cost Estimate
Gifts	_____	_____
	_____	_____
	_____	_____
	_____	_____
	_____	_____
	_____	_____
	_____	_____
	_____	_____

Favors Worksheet (Chapter 12)

Ideas: _____

_____

_____

Cost per person: _____

Contact: _____

Telephone: _____ Fax: _____ E-mail: _____

Hotel contact who will deliver favors to guests: _____

Notes: _____

_____

_____

_____

Floral Worksheet (Chapter 9)

Company: _____

Address: _____

Telephone: _____ Fax: _____ E-mail: _____

Type of flowers desired: _____

_____

Wedding colors: _____

Ceremony site flowers: _____

_____

Aisle cloth wanted? _____

Floor plan for ceremony: _____

_____

Floor plan for reception: _____

_____

Ideas for reception flowers: _____

_____

Centerpieces: _____

_____

Notes: _____

_____

_____

_____

_____

Invitations Worksheet (Chapter 11)

Company: _____

Address: _____

Telephone: _____ Fax: _____ E-mail: _____

Contact: _____

Discount available: _____ Paper number: _____

Quantity needed: _____ Ink color: _____

Style or theme: _____

Enclosures:

    Reception cards: _____

    Response cards and envelopes: _____

    Maps: _____

Accessories:

    Napkins: _____

    Informal notes: _____

    Toast glasses: _____

    Place cards: _____

    Programs: _____

    Matches: _____

    Cake knife: _____

    Scrolls: _____

    Favor ribbons: _____

    Thank you notes: _____

    Cake boxes or bags: _____

Notes: _____

_____

_____

_____

_____

Liquor Worksheet (Chapter 7)

Dealer: _____

Telephone: _____

Address: _____

Contact: _____

Requested:

     Open bar ____   Limited bar ____   Cash bar ____

Method of accountability: _____

Liquor requested: _____

_____

Number of bartenders needed: _____ Time for setup: _____

Notes: _____

_____

_____

_____

Musicians Worksheet (Chapter 9)

Company: _____

Address: _____

Telephone: _____ Fax: _____ E-mail: _____

Contact: _____

Contact phone number for the musicians: _____

Referred by: _____

Type of music (band, DJ, single instrument): _____

_____

Do they provide song list to choose from? _____

What is attire for reception? _____

How long will they play? _____ How many breaks will they take? _____

What are overtime charges? _____ Will they help with introductions and garter and bouquet toss? _____

Next appointment: _____

Notes: _____

_____

_____

_____

Photography Worksheet (Chapter 10)

Photographer: _____

Address: _____

Telephone: _____ Cell: _____ Fax: _____

Website: _____ E-mail: _____

Referred by: _____

Type of photography (portraiture, candid, photojournalistic, natural light): _____

_____

_____

Deposit paid (date): _____

Package plan (including time limit, overtime charges, charge for proofs, number of pictures, albums, etc.): _____

_____

_____

Next appointment: _____ Balance due: _____

Notes: _____

_____

_____

_____

_____

_____

Program Worksheet (Chapter 11)

Type of program desired: _____

Method of producing: _____

Self _____   Printer _____   Invitation company _____

Contact: _____

Telephone: _____ Fax: _____ E-mail: _____

Deadline for production: _____

Deposit paid (date): _____

Suggested wording: _____

_____

_____

_____

Notes: _____

_____

_____

_____

_____

Reception Site Worksheet (Chapter 4)

Reception facility: _____

Address: _____

Contact: _____

Telephone: _____ Fax: _____ E-mail: _____

Time for reception to begin: _____ Time for reception to end: _____

What the facility provides (linens, skirting, mike hookups): _____
_____
_____

Fee for site: _____ Deposit paid (date): _____

Floor plan layout (sketch here): _____
_____
_____
_____
_____

Appointments with manager: _____ Balance due: _____

Notes: _____
_____
_____
_____
_____

Rehearsal Dinner Worksheet (Chapter 6)

Place: _____

Address: _____

Telephone: _____ Fax: _____ E-mail: _____

Contact: _____

Time to begin: _____ Time to end: _____

Menu ideas: _____
_____
_____
_____

Meal price: _____ Bar charge: _____

Agenda ideas ("roast the couple," slide show, etc.): _____
_____
_____
_____

Equipment needed: _____

_____

_____

Invitations ordered: _____ Responses received: _____

Guest's Name	Address	# Attending
_____	_____	_____
_____	_____	_____
_____	_____	_____
_____	_____	_____
_____	_____	_____
_____	_____	_____
_____	_____	_____
_____	_____	_____
_____	_____	_____
_____	_____	_____
_____	_____	_____
_____	_____	_____

Notes: _____

_____

_____

Special Transportation Worksheet (Chapter 8)

Mode of transportation desired: _____

Contact: _____

Telephone: _____ Cell: _____

Referred by: _____

Contract used: _____

Contract/deposit returned (date): _____ Hours needed (time of day): _____

Special instructions/directions sent: _____

_____

_____

Notes: _____

_____

_____

Tuxedo Worksheet (Chapter 8)

Name of store: _____

Address: _____

Telephone: _____ Fax: _____ E-mail: _____

Salesperson: _____ Price: _____

Style number: _____ Color: _____

Tie/cummerbund/vest/shirt color: _____

Accessories: Shoes: _____ Gloves: _____

               Hats: _____ Other: _____

Deposit made:

Name	Phone Number	Paid
_____	_____	_____
_____	_____	_____
_____	_____	_____
_____	_____	_____

Notes: _____

_____

_____

Videography Worksheet (Chapter 10)

Company: _____

Address: _____

Telephone: _____ Fax: _____

Website: _____ E-mail: _____

Contact: _____

Referred by: _____

Type of video requested (edited or unedited): _____

_____

Attends rehearsal? _____ Number of cameras needed: _____

Music selection: _____

_____

Provides cordless microphone for groom: _____

Special effects used (baby pictures, credits, animation, fade in or out, etc): _____

_____

_____

Notes: _____

_____

_____

Wedding Budget Worksheet (Chapter 2)

Item	Estimate	Actual
Rings:		
Engagement ring	$_____	$_____
Bride's wedding ring	$_____	$_____
Groom's wedding ring	$_____	$_____
Other	$_____	$_____
Bridal consultant (name)		
_____	$_____	$_____
Other	$_____	$_____
Ceremony:		
Site rental fee	$_____	$_____
Officiant's fee	$_____	$_____
Ceremony assistants' fee	$_____	$_____
Other	$_____	$_____
Reception:		
Site rental fee	$_____	$_____
Food	$_____	$_____
Beverages	$_____	$_____
Service personnel	$_____	$_____
Party rentals (chairs, tables, linens, etc.)	$_____	$_____
Other	$_____	$_____
Wedding cake:		
Charge for cake	$_____	$_____
Delivery fee	$_____	$_____
Groom's cake	$_____	$_____
Other	$_____	$_____
Reception:		
Napkins	$_____	$_____
Personalized matches	$_____	$_____
Favors	$_____	$_____
Toasting goblets	$_____	$_____
Cake knife	$_____	$_____
Scrolls	$_____	$_____
Other	$_____	$_____
Bride's clothing:		
Gown	$_____	$_____
Headpiece and veil	$_____	$_____
Alterations	$_____	$_____

Item	Estimate	Actual
Bride's clothing (continued):		
Shoes	$_____	$_____
Gloves	$_____	$_____
Hose	$_____	$_____
Jewelry	$_____	$_____
Garter	$_____	$_____
Lingerie	$_____	$_____
Other	$_____	$_____
Photography:		
Engagement announcement photo	$_____	$_____
Wedding portrait	$_____	$_____
Wedding photographs	$_____	$_____
Wedding albums	$_____	$_____
Other	$_____	$_____
Videography:		
One camera	$_____	$_____
Two cameras	$_____	$_____
Three or more cameras	$_____	$_____
Fee for extra DVD	$_____	$_____
Editing charge	$_____	$_____
Other	$_____	$_____
Flowers:		
Ceremony flowers	$_____	$_____
Reception flowers	$_____	$_____
Personal flowers	$_____	$_____
Other	$_____	$_____
Wedding stationery:		
Invitations	$_____	$_____
Announcements	$_____	$_____
Reception cards	$_____	$_____
Response cards	$_____	$_____
Thank you notes	$_____	$_____
Informals	$_____	$_____
Maps:	$_____	$_____
Newsletters	$_____	$_____
Other	$_____	$_____
Music:		
Ceremony:		
Soloist	$_____	$_____
Organist/pianist	$_____	$_____

Item	Estimate	Actual
Reception	$_____	$_____
Other	$_____	$_____
Groom's clothing:		
Tuxedo/suit	$_____	$_____
Shirt	$_____	$_____
Tie	$_____	$_____
Vest/cummerbund	$_____	$_____
Shoes	$_____	$_____
Accessories	$_____	$_____
Other	$_____	$_____
Gifts:		
Attendants	$_____	$_____
Gifts to each other	$_____	$_____
Parents' Thank you gifts	$_____	$_____
Other	$_____	$_____
Transportation:		
Limousine	$_____	$_____
Parking	$_____	$_____
Other	$_____	$_____
Rehearsal dinner (included, even though traditionally paid for by groom's family):		
Food	$_____	$_____
Beverages	$_____	$_____
Service personnel	$_____	$_____
Room rental charge	$_____	$_____
Flowers/decorations	$_____	$_____
Other	$_____	$_____
Honeymoon:		
Hotel	$_____	$_____
Transportation	$_____	$_____
Tours	$_____	$_____
Meals	$_____	$_____
Passports	$_____	$_____
Traveler's checks	$_____	$_____
Other	$_____	$_____
Additional expenses:		
Marriage license	$_____	$_____
Invitation postage	$_____	$_____
Gratuities	$_____	$_____
Blood tests/physicals	$_____	$_____

Item	Estimate	Actual
Hair stylist	$_____	$_____
Makeup artist	$_____	$_____
Bubbles or petals	$_____	$_____
Other	$_____	$_____

Wedding Cake Worksheet (Chapter 7)

Baker: _____

Address: _____

Telephone: _____ Fax: _____ E-mail: _____

Price: _____ Delivery fee: _____ Deposit on cake pieces: _____

How to get items back to baker: _____ Number of servings: _____

Description of wedding cake: _____

_____

_____

Description of groom's cake: _____

_____

_____

Number of servings: _____

Notes: _____

_____

_____

Wedding Gown and Bridesmaids' Dresses Worksheet (Chapter 8)

Shops to visit: _____

_____

Referred by: _____

Date of appointments: _____

_____

Name of contact at shop: _____

Telephone: _____

Style of gown: _____

_____

Color selection: _____

Budgeted amount for gown and veil: _____

Budgeted amount for accessories: _____

    Bra: _____

    Slip: _____

    Shoes: _____

    Jewelry: _____

Deposit paid (date): _____

Payments to be made (dates): _____

Bridesmaids' dresses: _____

    Number of attendants: _____

    Color choices: _____

    Style of dresses: _____

    Cost of dresses: _____

    Cost of alterations: _____

Attendants' names, phone numbers, and addresses:

    1. _____

       _____

       _____

    2. _____

       _____

       _____

    3. _____

       _____

       _____

    4. _____

       _____

       _____

    5. _____

       _____

       _____

    6. _____

       _____

       _____

(Add more paper if needed.)

Next appointment: _____

Notes: _____

_____

_____

_____

_____

_____

What's Important to Us Worksheet (Chapter 2)

Number of guests: _____ Number of attendants: _____

Time of day: _____ Time of year: _____

Other (limousine, photography, videography, special items [hot air balloon, vintage cars], decorations, flowers [silk vs. fresh], and attire): _____

_____

_____

Reception:

- ☐ Cake and punch
- ☐ Hors d'oeuvres
- ☐ Buffet
- ☐ Sit-down dinner

- ☐ Open bar
- ☐ Limited bar
- ☐ Cash bar
- ☐ Champagne toast

- ☐ Music
- ☐ Dancing
- ☐ Favors

Other ideas: _____

_____

_____

_____

Who Pays for What? Worksheet (Chapter 2)

The Bride and Her Family:

- Wedding dress, headpiece, and accessories
- Ceremony site rental
- Bridal consultant
- Reception site rental
- Reception food and drink
- Ceremony flowers
- Reception flowers
- Groom's wedding ring
- Invitations, announcements, and enclosures
- Gift for the groom
- Gifts for the bridesmaids

The Groom and His Family:

- Bride's engagement and wedding rings
- Gift for the bride
- Formal wear rental
- Marriage license
- Officiant's fee

- Boutonnieres for the men in the wedding party
- Bride's bouquet
- Corsages for the mothers and grandmothers
- Gifts for the men in the wedding party
- Honeymoon
- Rehearsal dinner

The Wedding Party:

- Their wedding attire
- Accessories to go with the attire (shoes, headpieces)
- Gift for the bride and groom
- Transportation to the city (if out of town)

Notes: _____

_____

_____

_____

_____

_____

_____

Countdown to Your
Wedding Day

This handy checklist can help you stay on track in the months and weeks leading up to your wedding day. I suggest you read through the list completely (just disregard any items that don't apply to your wedding). Get a handle on what you need to do when and then, as each item is dealt with, you can check it off as done!

Six to Twelve Months Before the Wedding

- ☐ Announce your engagement.
- ☐ Plan the engagement party or make the announcement to the rest of your family and friends.
- ☐ Attend bridal shows.
- ☐ Talk with a bridal consultant/wedding coordinator. Make an appointment for a consultation.
- ☐ Together with both sets of parents, discuss wedding plans, including formality.
- ☐ Determine a budget.
- ☐ If you're sharing expenses, decide who is paying for what.
- ☐ Select a date and time for the wedding.
- ☐ Reserve the church or synagogue or other venue for the ceremony, and make an appointment with the officiant.
- ☐ If it will be a civil ceremony, call the officiant.
- ☐ Meet with the officiant.
- ☐ Ask friends and family to serve as wedding attendants.
- ☐ Start comparison shopping for services such as florist, caterer, photographer, and videographer.
- ☐ Select wedding rings, and make any necessary arrangements for engraving.
- ☐ Begin writing your guest lists.
- ☐ Gather ideas for reception: menu, beverages, entertainment, favors, and so on.
- ☐ Reserve your reception site.
- ☐ Reserve your vendors: caterer, photographer, videographer, florist, musicians, limo, and so on.
- ☐ Begin to plan the wedding ceremony and reception music.
- ☐ Register with department stores for bridal gift registry.
- ☐ Begin shopping and order your gown, veil and/or headpiece.

Five Months Before the Wedding

- ☐ Select and order attendants' dresses.
- ☐ Discuss honeymoon plans with your fiancé, and speak with a travel agent.
- ☐ Begin shopping for your wedding invitations, enclosure cards, thank you notes, and informal notes.
- ☐ Begin shopping for your wedding cake.
- ☐ Reserve blocks of rooms at hotels for out-of-town guests (include this information with the invitations).

Four Months Before the Wedding

- ☐ Select and order your wedding stationery: invitations, announcements, enclosures, informals, scrolls, napkins, and thank you notes.
- ☐ Get necessary travel documents (passport, birth certificate).
- ☐ Draw maps with directions to the ceremony and reception site for out-of-town guests.
- ☐ Make an appointment with the caterer or banquet manager to discuss your reception menu.
- ☐ Make an appointment with your bridal consultant to touch base and get your questions answered.

Three Months Before the Wedding

- [ ] Decide on a honeymoon destination, and call for reservations. (You might want to do this earlier if you're going to a popular honeymoon destination.)
- [ ] Begin making a list of clothing and other items you'll need for the honeymoon. Start shopping for those.
- [ ] Finalize your guest list, check for duplicates, and correct spelling and addresses.
- [ ] Review musical selections with your musicians.
- [ ] Arrange for an engagement picture for the newspaper.
- [ ] Make an appointment with the florist to discuss floral budget and floral decorations.
- [ ] Check with local authorities about requirements for marriage license and blood test.
- [ ] Begin addressing the inner and outer invitation envelopes.
- [ ] Complete honeymoon plans. Buy air or cruise tickets.

Two Months Before the Wedding

- [ ] Order the wedding cake and groom's cake.
- [ ] Have a physical examination, blood tests, and any required inoculations for foreign travel.
- [ ] Accompany groom to the formal wear shop, and choose formal attire for the male attendants.

Seven Weeks Before the Wedding

- [ ] Meet with the caterer or banquet manager, and firm up reception details. Ask for a banquet room floor plan.
- [ ] Consult a party rental store if equipment is needed at the reception.
- [ ] Schedule an appointment with the bridal consultant.
- [ ] Talk with musicians and review your selections.
- [ ] Make an appointment with your photographer for your formal bridal portrait.

Six Weeks Before the Wedding

- [ ] Call the church or synagogue and confirm the rehearsal date and time.
- [ ] Discuss music with the church organist and soloist.
- [ ] Plan the rehearsal dinner with the caterer.
- [ ] Visit the church and reception site and do a floor plan (if not done earlier).
- [ ] Have the males in the wedding party, including the fathers, rent their formal wear at the same store.
- [ ] If some male attendants are from out of town, have the local store call or e-mail them with the tux information and ask that they call or e-mail their measurements back to the store.
- [ ] If bridesmaids live out of town, arrange for their dresses to be sent to them for fittings and alterations.
- [ ] Order wedding programs.
- [ ] Order favors (if using).

Five Weeks Before the Wedding

- ☐ Mail all the invitations.
- ☐ Meet the florist and order your flowers. Take samples of fabric and pictures of your gown and attendants' gowns.
- ☐ Purchase or borrow bridal garter, guest book, pen, cake knife, and toasting glasses.
- ☐ Select and buy gifts for all attendants.

Four Weeks Before the Wedding

- ☐ Prepare the wedding announcement for the local newspaper.
- ☐ All invitations should be in the mail.
- ☐ Make an appointment with your hair stylist and makeup artist to try out makeup and hairstyles for your wedding day. Be sure to make the appointments for the wedding day, too.
- ☐ Finalize rehearsal dinner arrangements.
- ☐ Finalize reception arrangements.
- ☐ Check with attendants regarding their accessories.
- ☐ Wrap attendants' gifts and have them ready to present.
- ☐ Make an appointment for your gown's final fitting.
- ☐ Begin recording invitation acceptances and regrets.
- ☐ Begin addressing announcement envelopes.
- ☐ Select wedding gifts for each other.
- ☐ Arrange for transportation of the wedding party to the wedding and reception.
- ☐ Discuss the ceremony with the officiant.
- ☐ Make a seating plan for the rehearsal dinner and reception.
- ☐ Write place cards for the reception (if using).
- ☐ Decide whether you'll use a receiving line.
- ☐ If you're moving to another town after the wedding, make arrangements with the movers.

Three Weeks Before the Wedding

- ☐ Have your final gown-fitting.
- ☐ Notify all participants of rehearsal date, time, and place.
- ☐ Have your formal portrait taken.
- ☐ Check on honeymoon tickets and reservations.
- ☐ Set up a table to display your wedding gifts.
- ☐ Record gifts and continue to send thank you notes.
- ☐ Get the marriage license.
- ☐ Confirm transportation to the ceremony and reception.
- ☐ Attend showers given in your honor.
- ☐ Arrange for the bridesmaids' luncheon.
- ☐ Ask a friend to handle the wedding gifts at the reception.
- ☐ Make arrangements for the gifts to be taken from the reception to your home or to storage.
- ☐ Hire a house-sitter for the rehearsal and wedding day for your home, your parents' home, and your fiancé's home.
- ☐ Ask someone to be the guest book attendant.
- ☐ Check with cleaners about preserving your gown.
- ☐ Assign someone to take your gown to the cleaners.
- ☐ Pick up tickets and confirm reservations for the honeymoon.

Two Weeks Before the Wedding

☐ Finalize hotel arrangements for out-of-town guests.

☐ Plan a "welcome" package for out-of-town guests to be in their hotel rooms when they arrive.

☐ Send your photograph and wedding announcement to the newspaper.

☐ Check on accessories for the groom and male attendants.

☐ Give addressed and stamped announcements to someone to mail the day after the wedding.

☐ Follow up with guests who have not returned their response card. You must have an accurate count for the caterer.

☐ Meet with your bridal consultant to go over all the final details.

One Week Before the Wedding

☐ Eat right and get plenty of rest this week!

☐ Give the caterer a guaranteed count for the reception.

☐ Double-check all service providers: florist, photographer, caterer, church, and so on. Or have your bridal consultant take care of these calls.

☐ Pay balances due on services required before the wedding.

☐ Have money or checks in envelopes for your consultant to hand to the organist, soloist, musicians, minister, and anyone who needs to be paid the day of the wedding.

☐ Attend the bridesmaids' luncheon.

☐ Remind everyone of the time and place of the rehearsal.

☐ Pack for the honeymoon.

☐ Give gifts to your attendants (if not planned for rehearsal dinner).

☐ Spend some quiet time with your family.

☐ Have "something old, new, borrowed, and blue" ready.

☐ Explain any special seating to your bridal consultant.

☐ Attend the bachelorette party (not the night before the wedding!).

Two Days Before the Wedding

☐ Check the weather conditions for the wedding day, and make adjustments if needed.

☐ Lay out everything you'll need to dress for the wedding in one place at home.

☐ Your bridal consultant should provide a care package: safety pins, thread, bobby pins, hairspray, soft drinks, juice, crackers, and more for your use.

☐ Be sure the cars involved are clean and have gas.

One Day Before the Wedding

- ☐ Attend the rehearsal.

- ☐ Be sure you and your groom are comfortable with the rehearsal and have no questions.

- ☐ If you're leaving for your honeymoon directly from the reception, place your luggage in the car you'll be driving and lock it.

- ☐ *Relax*. Take a hot bath. Have a glass of warm milk or hot tea, and get a good night's rest.

The Big Day!

- ☐ Have your bridal consultant get your gown, veil, and/or bridesmaids' gowns from the bridal shop and take them directly to the ceremony site (if the shop doesn't deliver).

- ☐ Eat a good breakfast—something that will last. You want to include protein items and some bread items (for energy). You might be too nervous to eat closer to the wedding time.

- ☐ Give yourself plenty of time to get ready. Don't rush! Enjoy this time. You may even indulge and have a makeup artist and hair stylist come to the ceremony site to apply your makeup and do your hair.

- ☐ Your consultant should be sure that anything belonging to you that needs to go from the church to the reception will be taken there, or assign this task to a reliable friend.

- ☐ *Enjoy this day!* You've planned well, and now you can relax.

Best wishes for a lifetime of happiness!